MW01680728

Quaker Profiles

Judy Edgerton

Quaker Profiles

Jewell Conrad Edgerton

A Memorial Volume Dedicated to the Author

Edited
and with an Introduction and Profile of the Author
by William Edgerton

Celo Valley Books
Burnsville, North Carolina

Copies of *Quaker Profiles* may be obtained from:

Quaker Hill Bookstore, 101 Quaker Hill Drive, Richmond, Indiana 47374-1980; telephone: 800-537-8838.

Friends General Conference Bookstore, 1216 Arch Street, 2B, Philadelphia, Pennsylvania 19107; telephone: 800-966-4556.

Pendle Hill Bookstore, 338 Plush Mill Road, Wallingford, Pennsylvania 19086-6099; telephone: 800-742-3150.

Library of Congress Catalog Card Number 95-67546
ISBN 0-923687-34-3

Printed in the U.S.A.

TABLE OF CONTENTS

INTRODUCTION

The first thirty-seven of the Quaker profiles in this book were originally published in the newsletter of Bloomington Friends Meeting between April 1990, when Jewell Conrad Edgerton (known to her family and friends as Judy) became its editor, and December 23, 1993, when she died unexpectedly of complications following open-heart surgery. She had planned to retire as editor of the newsletter sometime in 1994 after profiling the rest of the meeting members, concluding the series with my profile and her own, written by each other.

In 1991 when the first sixteen of these profiles came out in a limited edition entitled *Quaker Profiles, Volume I*, readers from elsewhere remarked about the interesting group of people we have in Bloomington Friends Meeting. Judy would always reply that everybody's spiritual journey makes an interesting story — whereupon I would always add, "Provided you have a Judy to tell it." Like a gifted painter whose portraits can open our eyes to qualities a camera cannot record, Judy Edgerton in her Quaker profiles has not only aroused the interest of readers in other parts of the country. She has also reacquainted those of us in Bloomington Meeting with fellow members whom we thought we had known well for years.

Death frustrated Judy's plans after retirement to reprint the remaining profiles as *Quaker Profiles, Volume II*. Instead, in this memorial volume dedicated to her, I now publish all the thirty-seven profiles that she wrote, along with a thirty-eighth of Judy herself written by the only person on earth who knew her well enough to write it — her husband of fifty-eight years.

Judy developed the profiles from interviews. Before the first interview she would give candidates a short list of questions about their life and the course of their spiritual journey. The interview would ordinarily take place at the Edgerton home over lunch and would sometimes last two or three hours, with Judy taking many pages of notes.

The interviews were themselves a meaningful religious experience for many of those profiled. Under Judy's thoughtful, gentle questioning, they would turn into a kind of spiritual stocktaking, full of meaning for both author and subject. "She saw people for what they were," said one profiled Friend, "but managed to find the positive aspects of everyone."

Judy would then spend two or three days mulling over the material she had collected, looking for a key idea that could serve to tie the whole sketch together. Once she had found it, she would write fairly quickly, first in longhand, then revising as she typed the final draft. Her last step was always to send a copy to the persons profiled, asking them to correct any errors of fact.

What emerged were beautifully written accounts of each subject's life and spiritual journey. The profiles grew in length and depth over the three and a half years in which they were written. The first seven occupied only a page each in the Meeting newsletter, and are mainly factual. At that point, however, Judy hit her stride. The subsequent profiles are longer and considerably more powerful.

These Friends' stories are all vivid, richly detailed, sometimes humorous or quirky, often very moving. The voice that tells them is unwaveringly affectionate and wise. The result is a collection of informal essays that are at once engrossing examples of narrative art and lovely devotional readings. In each profile an adroitly woven narrative thread knits together what amounts to a skilled storyteller's meditation on psychology, personal history, and spiritual seeking.

Bloomington is one of many American Quaker meetings that have sprung up during this century in college or university communities. It was founded in February 1950 by six people associated with Indiana University. Today the meeting has about fifty resident adult members, and total attendance at meetings for worship ranges from fifty to seventy-five. For us the term "campus meeting" is merely a figure of speech, because our meetinghouse is located a good three miles from the Indiana University campus. The reality of our association with the university, however, can be seen in at least three ways: in the more than a dozen faculty and staff families among meeting members, in the number of students — particularly graduate students and their families — who spend several years in our midst as meeting attenders or as sojourning members from their home meetings, and in the number of Friends now in meetings all over the United States who have spent some time in our meeting as students or as young faculty members before settling elsewhere. Our state of perpetual change is reflected in the profiles published here. They are presented in the form in which they first appeared in the newsletter, including their original dates of publication. Among the thirty-eight subjects of these profiles, three students have completed their studies and moved away, and our Irish member and his wife have just returned to Ireland. In the whole group there have been three marriages, one divorce, one withdrawal from the meeting, and one death.

The paths that led these thirty-eight Quakers to Bloomington began with their births in fourteen states and six foreign countries. Their previous religious experiences were linked with more than a dozen Christian denominations and with fifteen yearly meetings in the Society of Friends. For all the geographic and religious cosmopolitanism, however, and for all the membership's academic ties, it would be a mistake to assume that the whole group inhabits an ivory tower attached to Indiana University. Among members and attenders who live in the real world are several health-care professionals, a farmer, a cabinetmaker, a carpenter, a metalworker, an architect, a retired heating and air conditioning specialist, and a graduate of the University of Wisconsin School of Agriculture who worked for forty-five years as an announcer at the International Livestock Show in Chicago.

From the date of its founding, Bloomington Monthly Meeting has been an active member of Western Yearly Meeting. When we purchased a house in 1966 to serve as our permanent meeting place, the Yearly Meeting helped us with a loan and with outright grants to transform the dwelling house into an attractive Quaker meetinghouse, with a characteristic Quaker veranda running across the front and a beautiful meeting room built onto one end of the structure. Even though we are one of the few unprogrammed, non-pastoral meetings in Western Yearly Meeting, we were welcomed from the first and were encouraged to share in the work of the Yearly Meeting.

The decision to publish these profiles in book form was prompted mainly by two considerations. The first is the sheer drama in them, involving personal joys and sorrows, adventures and misadventures, in more than twenty countries on four continents. The second is the encouragement that these thirty-eight spiritual journeys may offer to other seekers after the meaning of life and death. In the narrative skill, spiritual richness, and quiet power of these profiles, local readers have found an appeal that clearly reflects but also transcends their specifically Quaker context. I offer them here in the expectation that a wider readership, Quaker and non-Quaker alike, will also find joy and strength in them.

Most Quakers are aware that one thing setting us apart from some other religious groups is our acknowledgment that the Society of Friends is not the source of all spiritual truth. It is like one of the spokes in an enormous wheel whose center is ultimate spiritual reality, or God. The closer we get to God, the closer we get to each other.

— William Edgerton

QUAKER PROFILE No. 1:

Janice Clevenger

Have you seen her on the back bench on the south side of Bloomington Friends meeting room during worship on First-days, a quiet figure in meditation? And have you seen her on the stage with the local Civic Theater — a changed personality, bringing to life a fictitious character?

These are two sides to Janice Clevenger, but there is much more.

She is a real Hoosier, born in Bloomington (by way of an Indianapolis hospital), and the second of two daughters of Cyrus and Mary Beth Clevenger. The family moved to Martinsville for a brief time, then to Columbus, Indiana, where Janice graduated from high school. They returned to Bloomington in 1947 to the home on South Henderson Street where Janice still lives. She comes from a Presbyterian background, and became a member of Bloomington Friends Meeting in its infancy in 1952. Her mother attended the meeting with Janice, rendering valued service in working with the children in First-day school.

Janice's first contact with Quakers was as a student at Earlham College in Richmond, Indiana. In her sophomore year she took time out to go to art school in Indianapolis, and then became Earlham's first major in fine arts. Work with Quaker outreach began in 1951 when she participated in the International Work Camp Program in Germany with the American Friends Service Committee. She learned about the work of Friends in Japan when she attended a summer session at Pendle Hill, in Wallingford, Pennsylvania, in 1956.

Experience there included a Quaker leadership tour during which she became acquainted with the work of leaders in the Society of Friends through visits to several yearly meetings.

In 1957 Janice was asked to teach at Tokyo Friends School in Japan by the Japan Committee of Philadelphia Yearly Meeting (now International Outreach). Her eyes brighten as she recalls the boat trip to Japan and her first sight of snow-covered Mount Fuji from Yokohama harbor on the fourth of February of that year. She increased her teaching skills and her East-West interpretative ability by returning to the United States and obtaining an M.A. in Far Eastern Languages and Literatures from the University of Michigan in 1960. After an interim year of teaching at Baltimore Friends School, she resumed teaching at Tokyo Friends School. She became steeped in Japanese culture and customs, and a tea ceremony in costume given on a trip home at the Bloomington Friends meetinghouse is remembered with pleasure by this writer.

In 1969, Janice became Friend in Residence for Seoul Friends Meeting in Korea under the auspices of the Friends World Committee for Consultation. While there she also taught English at Hankuk University of Foreign Studies. Among the performances she directed as head of dramatics at the university were Gilbert and Sullivan's *Pinafore* and *Pirates of Penzance.*

Janice returned home to Bloomington in 1974 and now lives together with her sister Sarah Clevenger, a retired professor, at their family home. She sells her handmade mother dolls with nursing babies through ads in *Mothering* magazine. The sisters jointly own and manage rental properties and cooperate in running their print shop, Pixel Place, featuring computer sales and services.

Janice remains a sojourning member of Tokyo Friends Meeting and maintains contact with people there as well as in Seoul. Since returning to Bloomington Meeting, she has served on various committees, including Ministry and Counsel, as time allows, and she speaks out of the silence from time to time in meeting for worship.

— Judy Edgerton, April 1990

QUAKER PROFILE No. 2:

Malika Richards

Anyone who has not met and talked with Malika Richards has missed a rare opportunity. She is in Hawaii as this profile is being written, but look for her at Bloomington Friends meeting for worship after classes begin at Indiana University for the fall semester, 1990. If you think of her as the slender, smiling blonde May Queen on the Earlham College campus, you will have no trouble recognizing her!

The Earlham students who elected Malika as their own queen a few years ago may not have known that she was already a queen to her parents, who gave her the Arabic name that translates into English as "queen" when she was born in Kuwait (on the Persian Gulf) thirty-one years ago. Malika's friendly, modest manner belies a cosmopolitan background beginning in the Middle East and extending as an adult to the Far East. She is a third-generation birthright Friend, both parents being Quaker. Her mother was educated in an English Quaker school. Her American father, a physician, and all of his family are Westtown School graduates. One of seven children, Malika sees her scattered family as often as possible. An ocean divides those in London and in Edinburgh, Scotland, from Malika and the rest of the family here in the United States.

Eight of Malika's early childhood years were spent in Edinburgh. During her preteen and high school years she lived first in Chestnut Hill (Philadelphia) and then in Troy, in northern Pennsylvania. After that she chose Earlham College in Richmond, Indiana, and took a major in human development and social relations with emphasis on sociology and psychology. Her interest in the Far East began as an undergraduate in a humanities class in which the professor made impressive use of a videotape he had made in Japan. Malika spent her junior year there, taking advantage of the opportunity to learn the Japanese language while fulfilling Earlham College's requirement as a student teacher.

The Japanese experience was a valuable introduction to the Orient before she joined the Peace Corps for work in Thailand. In March 1982, just three months after graduation at mid-year, Malika was in Bangkok, Thailand's capital. Her arrival there coincided with the bicentennial year of its founding. She taught English to junior high school students there for three years, and then at Chulalongkorn University for two years. Malika says the university, named for its founder, King Chulalongkorn (Rama V), is the oldest in the country.

In addition to Japanese, Malika now had learned the Thai language. She traveled in mainland China in 1982 and 1987 and spent two summers on the island of Taiwan. These experiences gave her yet another Oriental language, Chinese. Her purpose in being in Honolulu, Hawaii, at this present moment, to quote Malika herself, is "to get background information, through research, in Thai economic development and foreign direct-investment theory, in a seminar-like setting." She is joining a study group, the East-West Center, set up and funded by the United States Congress, which lasts from May to mid-August 1990.

Malika has completed all her work toward the M.B.A. in the School of Business at Indiana University. She is now completing her course work for the Ph.D. and expects to be ready for the required field examination in the fall of 1991. Meanwhile, she will continue to teach senior undergraduates at the Business School in two courses entitled Strategic Management, which she describes as "vision . . . planning . . . composite level strategy . . ." At a time when American businesses are expanding more and more into foreign countries, our Quaker "queen" will be entering the business world as one of the few Americans prepared in both business administration and the languages and cultures of the Far East.

— Judy Edgerton, May 1990

QUAKER PROFILE No. 3:

Amy Schutt

We see Amy Schutt as wife and mother, mingling easily among children and adults at the meetinghouse on Sunday mornings, along with husband Robert and four-year-old son Thomas (Rob and Tom). She is a birthright Friend — of Norwegian ancestry from her father, Ralph Slotten, and English Quaker ancestry from her mother, Martha Calvert Slotten. Her mother's family tree has its roots in the Quakerism of George Fox's day in the 1600s. Her maternal grandmother's home was in Carthage, Indiana, and her mother grew up in Selma, Ohio, in the Green Plain Friends Meeting.

Amy's own religious upbringing was ecumenical in a college community, where her mother was an archivist and her father professor of the history of religions at Dickinson College in Carlisle, Pennsylvania, near the state capital, Harrisburg. She, her brother, and their parents attended a church at the college made up of people of various Protestant denominations. In addition, they often worshiped with a church calling itself the All-People's Church, consisting of Catholics, Protestants, and Jews who met in the homes of members. At the same time, Amy was a member of Harrisburg Monthly Meeting (unprogrammed), and just before moving to Bloomington she and Rob were members of First Friends Meeting in Indianapolis.

Amy was a history major at Earlham College in Richmond, Indiana, but she did not meet Rob in history class. They met in a class in romantic literature, where they were evidently serious students, for they were married in 1981 after their graduation.

The wife-and-mother Amy that we see is only one important piece that seems to fit well into the personal mosaic that is Amy's life. She is now a candidate for the Ph.D. degree in colonial history at Indiana University, having recently passed her qualifying examination. Research for her dissertation on the work of a religious sect that has an early history of pacifism fits neatly into the mosaic. Although not as well known as the colonial Quakers for their effort to deal peaceably and respectfully with Native Americans, Amy's research reveals that the Moravian Brethren — a term they used for themselves — took a similar nonviolent approach.

While taking classes in the history department, Amy has for the past five years been employed half-time as managing editor of the *History of Education Quarterly*, with offices at Indiana University. From 1983 to 1985 she served as assistant editor of the *Indiana Magazine of History*. Preceding that experience, she was editorial assistant at the Indiana Historical Society in Indianapolis.

As this profile goes to press, Amy is devoting two weeks to the study of old German handwriting at the Moravian College and Seminary in Bethlehem, Pennsylvania, having learned modern German at Earlham. This is in preparation for reading unpublished German Moravian historical documents from colonial times. Meanwhile, Rob and Tom are settling into the family's newly purchased home at 504 East Dixie Street in Bloomington, where they had moved during the same week that Amy left for Bethlehem.

A last important piece in the mosaic is Amy's active participation in the religious life of the Bloomington Friends Meeting. She has been appointed by monthly meeting to be clerk of the Religious Education committee for the year beginning in July.

So there we have the whole six-piece mosaic: daughter, wife, mother, professional in historical journalism, scholar in religious history, and Quaker who will be using her talents for a most important job in our meeting.

— Judy Edgerton, June 1990

QUAKER PROFILE No. 4:

Nicola Brogden

How to catch the essence of a personality and transfer it to paper? One thing is certain: it is not Quaker gray. We have in mind our English import, Nicola Jean Brogden. Lovely to look at and a privilege to know, she adds another dimension to the already varied design of our Friends meeting.

Upon learning that Nicola's B.A. degree from Bradford College in England is in art and design, we say, "Of course!" Finding that she used these skills to design toys for the education of retarded children is again no surprise. She spent the eighteenth year of her life working with other Quaker volunteers at a home for the severely retarded in Austria. In England she used her skills to launch her career by teaching pottery and weaving to retarded adults. Then she worked in London at a government-sponsored charity, a home for severely retarded teens and preteens where the program was in transition, as these young people were being moved from a large facility into small homes in neighborhood settings.

Nicola's father, Geoffrey Brogden, was undoubtedly the role model who inspired Nicola to do her year of service in Austria and choose a career helping to build skills and confidence in retarded persons. He has been in social-service work all his adult life, has trained social workers out of his own wide experience, and is now teaching sociology in a prison.

Both Nicola's father and her mother, Iris Washbourne Brogden, were evacuated from London to the countryside as children during World War II. It seems natural that they chose to live with their children, Nicola and her sister Liz, in the peace and quiet of a small town, Needham Market, near the North Sea. There the family was part of Ipswich Friends Meeting, which is similar in size and attendance to our Bloomington Meeting.

According to Nicola, she and the other children in Ipswich Meeting spent more time in the adjoining park feeding the ducks than learning Quaker history. As the children grew older and joined their elders inside, they heard the Bible, as well as other religious literature, read aloud in meeting for worship. A table placed in the center of the meeting room at Ipswich Meeting holds these books for use by worshipers, who select and read aloud passages appropriate to the messages they bring to the meeting. Copies of the Book of Discipline are placed conveniently near each pew. Nicola describes this center table as often holding a bouquet of flowers. She also remembers hymns and prayers she learned as a child, which were a part of the opening of each school day in all English public schools.

Nicola and her family are vegetarians, as are twenty-five percent of the English population today, she tells us. She continued her association with various groups of Quakers as a young adult, and it was at one of these gatherings in 1986 that an event took place which she says changed her life. That event was meeting the American Ken Bardonner. The occasion was a gathering of Friends held at High Leigh, in Hertfordshire, north of London. Ken was at the meeting by mere chance while on a vacation tour that included England. He and Nicola met at a square dance, a recreational part of the meetings. He persuaded her to return with him to Indiana and became her husband. They still go folk dancing every Wednesday evening here in Bloomington.

Coming home with Ken was not without its frustrations for Nicola; mountainous red tape and ferrying back and forth by plane to England to keep her tourist visa became the routine until she obtained her fiancée visa. Stepping into August heat on arriving in New York was Nicola's first big surprise. Although she already had a driver's license, the presence of so many cars and the need in the States to rely on them — in the absence of a good public inter-city rail system — required some adjustment. Leaving family and friends and knowing no one here in the States was also hard at first. Finally, her sister Liz came over on a visit and Nicola began to settle in. Last summer (1989) Nicola and Ken realized their dream of going back and spending some time in England. And only a few weeks ago the visit was returned; Nicola was able to introduce her parents to Bloomington and our Friends meeting.

Bloomingtonians of all ages, from preschool to senior citizen, take pleasure in making artwork under Nicola's guidance as part of the Parks and Recreation summer program. Ken and Nicola work hard at taking care of the environment. Along with their gardening, they have planted more than one hundred trees on their acreage. Nicola is here to stay, and we are blessed.

— Judy Edgerton, July 1990

QUAKER PROFILE No. 5:

Rachel Day

Two young people from Bloomington Friends Meeting, Ruth and Rachel Day, believe in preparation for making youthful dreams come true. The daughters of Mark and Dorothy Day, Ruth came to Bloomington and to this Friends meeting at age one and Rachel was born in Bloomington. Each of them will be leaving at the end of this month for the colleges of their choice: Ruth to Carleton College in Northfield, Minnesota, where she is in her second year, and Rachel to Smith College in Northampton, Massachusetts, to begin her freshman year. Natural sibling rivalries have faded into adult reminiscences; Rachel and Ruth plan to keep in close touch with each other and with their parents by the use of computers with modems, high school graduation gifts from parents Dorothy and Mark.

Rachel has shown her versatility and organizational skills in her college preparation at Bloomington North High School by taking a heavy and varied course load, which included four years of science, mathematics, English, and French, and three years of social science and music. Extracurricular activities included three years of singing with the North High School concert choir and more than nine years of piano. Ballet lessons resulted in five years of dancing in the annual Indiana University *Nutcracker* performances. She also enjoyed her association with the young people's theater group, Acting Up, playing Anna in *The King and I.*

With this solid background, Rachel has chosen music and Italian as a double major at Smith College. She will take singing lessons in order to learn the proper use of her unusually beautiful and powerful natural voice. She will study the French, German, and Italian languages, these being mandatory for a student of voice. She started both Italian and vocal training at Indiana University during the past academic year, her senior year in high school. She is already thinking ahead to an advanced degree in music education after completing her undergraduate studies.

At Friends meeting we have had the opportunity of observing firsthand Rachel's energy and adaptability as she takes charge of young children while their parents attend various meetings. Her experience in the Society of Friends goes beyond her home meeting here in Bloomington. During four summers she has participated in Western Yearly Meeting's Quaker Haven summer camp program at Syracuse, Indiana (near Goshen). She was a camper in 1987 and 1988. She spent a week as counselor at Quaker Haven in 1989 and also during July of this year for Pioneer camp (grades five and six). She values these experiences, reporting that the organizers choose a theme for each week, with Bible study every morning in addition to the usual recreational activities such as swimming, crafts, etc. She has been a Young Friends representative on the Board on Christian Ministries and Evangelism of Western Yearly Meeting for two years, and during a part of that time she volunteered her services as recording clerk.

After having spent her childhood and teen years with Indiana Quakers, Rachel will broaden her experience in the Society of Friends this year at Smith College by attending the Mt. Toby Monthly Meeting (New England Yearly Meeting) in Amherst, Massachusetts.

This has evolved into Rachel's page. In September, we promise to have Ruth's profile.

— Judy Edgerton, August 1990

QUAKER PROFILE No. 6:

Ruth Day

Crossing oceans and learning languages while becoming acquainted with other peoples and their different cultures are a part of everyday life for Ruth Day and her family. Among the four of them, including sister Rachel and parents Dorothy and Mark, they now have seven languages. We might add an eighth one, computer literacy, for they are all skilled in the language of bits and bytes. Ruth remembers clearly when, between the age of six and eight, she went with her family to live in Saudi Arabia.

Naturally Ruth was excited one day, while going down the hall at Bloomington North High School, when she heard an announcement come over the loudspeaker about a student foreign-exchange program, Congress-Bundestag. The program is set up by agreement between the United States and German governments and organized under the sponsorship of the United States Information Agency. With a good all-round academic record and three years of German study, Ruth's acceptance was assured. She became one of three hundred high school students from across the United States to spend a year abroad from July 1988 to July 1989.

Ruth was in a group of 180 young people whose exchange was managed by the Youth For Understanding agency. After spending a month of orientation in Berlin she was assigned to a host family in the city of Osnabrück, which is located in Lower Saxony between Cologne and Hamburg. Becoming a third "daughter" in a family of four where both parents were teachers, Ruth found the wide-ranging family conversations stimulating. Life in a new country with a different family was a learning experience for Ruth but also for her host family. They in turn wanted to know their American "daughter" in depth, including her religious life. So our Ruth from the Bloomington Friends Meeting found herself to be a kind of ambassador for Friends, answering searching questions by people who had never heard of Quakers.

Ruth's background and training in music gave her a natural way of participating in German community life: she sang in a Lutheran church choir. She took a full program at the *Gymnasium*, which included religion — a regular part of the curriculum in Germany, where there is no sharp division between church and state.

Ruth observed that students tend to be better informed in more areas than young people at a similar level in American high schools. German students get a good basic education, with apparently no bias against rote memorization, before being admitted by examination to one of three types of secondary schools: the *Hauptschule* and *Realschule* for learning crafts and technical skills, and the *Gymnasium* to get a liberal education and prepare for the university, where they will immediately concentrate on a specialty. Ruth said that her most enjoyable experiences in Germany were the free exchanges of ideas under the skilled leadership of the *Gymnasium* faculty. Thus it was not only in her host family that she was confronted about her own religious convictions. The classroom setting afforded opportunities for exploration of philosophical and religious ideas as well as for lively discussion of such subjects as politics and international affairs.

When Ruth arrived back in the United States, she was chosen to speak in Washington, D.C., about her experiences before a group that included Indiana Senator Richard Lugar (a member of the Foreign Relations Committee), the German ambassador, a representative of the United States Information Agency, and both the returning Americans and the German exchange students leaving this country for home. Knowing that the videotaped speech was to be broadcast by television back in Germany, Ruth gave it in the German language.

A whole year has now gone by since the shock of suddenly plunging into the cold sea of cultural differences. As a young adult, in addition to being a birthright Quaker, Ruth has become a convinced Friend. She describes her feeling in meeting for worship as one of being peaceful and says, "I feel at home in meeting, and cared for. It's hard to describe. It's down-to-earth and yet I feel uplifted at the same time." She says that her sensitivity to and empathy with other people is attributable to the influence of her parents and to the Friends meeting.

As we write, Ruth is beginning her sophomore year at Carleton College in Northfield, Minnesota. She has been appointed to serve as a teaching associate in German, which is her area of concentration. Grandparents Ted and Bettyclaire Day, attenders at our Friends meeting, moved here in order to be near their son and his family. They drove Ruth to Carleton College at the same time that parents Dorothy and Mark were driving in the opposite direction to take Rachel to Smith College in Northampton, Massachusetts. We look forward to seeing all of them in Friends meeting when schedules allow trips home.

— Judy Edgerton, September 1990

QUAKER PROFILE No. 7:

Ethel Hobson Auf der Heyde

One would probably not expect a convinced Friend to be the result of an experience in a military camp. Yet that is where Ethel Hobson Auf der Heyde made her choice during the two years she spent at Fort Leavenworth in Kansas, where veterans were being briefed for reentry into civilian life after the Korean War. She was at the camp with her husband, William Auf der Heyde, D.D.S., who was on the dental staff. The subject of religion came up in philosophical discussion at a Great Books club meeting composed of officers, staff, and spouses. Someone in the group asked the question, What Christian church is closest to the way Christ taught? The answer came from a member of perhaps the best known military family in this century — Barbara Eisenhower, wife of John Eisenhower and daughter-in-law of General and President Dwight D. Eisenhower. She answered, "Quakers are the closest to the way Christ taught."

As a result of this experience, Ethel decided to learn more about Quakers than she already knew from her former contacts with Friends, particularly a Quaker college roommate. Ethel has spoken in meeting for worship about this friend of more than fifty years, Libby (Elizabeth) Walton, who "never criticized anyone, always saw the best in everyone," and who made theirs the "gathering room for many students." Perhaps then, and certainly in retrospect years later when Ethel joined the Society of Friends, she felt that Libby's "lovely attitude" in her day-to-day living was her unconscious witness as a Quaker.

When Ethel returned from Fort Leavenworth to her suburban Philadelphia home, she began attending the Gwynedd Friends Meeting only two miles away, where she and husband William were warmly welcomed. Their three children already felt at home in the meeting, because they had gone to weekday kindergarten in the meetinghouse. Each member of the family wrote a letter requesting membership and saying why they wished to join the Society of Friends. People still remember the smiles all around when eleven-year-old Billy Auf der Heyde gave as his reason: "Quakers are thrifty." He told his mother later that he was thinking of the elaborate and expensive lighting he had seen in another church.

Ethel gives credit to someone in Gwynedd meeting whom she describes as a "wonderful Friend" for making their entrance into the fellowship easy and warm. She appreciates time spent in the home of Eliza Foulke and her husband, dedicated Friends who had lived and worked in Japan. In their home she learned about Quakerism through personal contact and relaxed conversation, without the formality or the aid of books. Gwynedd Meeting's membership was around 150, large in comparison to some unprogrammed meetings, but Ethel describes a closeness and caring for one another which existed despite the size. She tells us that there is an oak tree on the grounds of the meeting which they call the William Penn Oak, because it was there when the meeting was established in 1691. (William Penn founded Philadelphia in 1681.) Like the roots of the great tree, the roots of that meeting have historic depth, giving the meeting its own long-established character and at the same time nurturing new life.

Ethel retains membership in the Gwynedd Meeting, but she has been very much a part of our Bloomington meeting for the past thirteen years. Daughter Andrea (Anne) Finley and her family live in Bloomington near the Auf der Heyde parents. Son Billy may remain a "thrifty Quaker" at heart, but he now belongs to another church in Colorado. Undoubtedly we will again see daughter Susan and her husband David Valentine and their children at meeting the next time they visit from their home in Ketchiken, Alaska. David and Susan have remained Friends even though there is no meeting in their vicinity; they use material from Philadelphia Yearly Meeting and hold their own Quaker meetings in their home.

Ethel is a clinical dietitian. She had a year's internship at Philadelphia General Hospital and practiced her profession at the Lankenau Hospital. She grew up in Crescentville and Jenkintown, both suburbs north of Philadelphia. She is a graduate of Hood College in Frederick, Maryland. Husband Bill practiced dentistry in Lansdowne, Pennsylvania, except for his two years as a dentist for the United States armed services at Fort Leavenworth.

It is a long way in miles from William Penn's historic city and the long-established Gwynedd Meeting to our relatively new and ever-changing Friends meeting in the onetime pioneer territory of Bloomington. To our good fortune, Friends Ethel and William have made the transition.

— Judy Edgerton, October 1990

QUAKER PROFILE No. 8:

Russell Comingore

Russell Comingore's Quaker heritage goes back more than two hundred years, through his mother, to England and Ireland. The area where he was born and grew up, in and around Paoli, Indiana, was settled by 217 Quakers from eastern North Carolina. They came in the year 1811, five years before Indiana became a state. These pioneers were part of the original colonial east-coast Carolinians. Russell's ever-so-great grandfather, Owen Lindley, had already visited the new Indiana territory on a scouting trip in 1807 and thought the type of soil and topography was similar enough to make adjustment easy. Owen Lindley's uncle, Jonathan Lindley, sold a profitable turpentine-production business in Orange County, North Carolina, in order to make possible the emigration of the whole group to virgin land. They named the large new Indiana tract after the place they had left (Orange County), and their leader, Jonathan Lindley, laid out the town of Paoli as it is today. Three separate Friends meetings were subsequently established: Beech Grove, Newberry, and Lick Creek. In 1892 Lick Creek set up Paoli Friends Meeting. All four of them still exist today.

With so much Quaker family history in his background, Quakerism could seem easy for Russell, but he does not take it for granted. He is in the Quaker tradition as an individualist in his thinking, and says, "I am opinionated, but I try not to be too hasty and to keep an open mind. After all, Quakers come in many different shapes, sizes, talents, and points of view."

If he is "opinionated," as he says of himself, these opinions are grounded in a knowledge of the Bible, as were the religious convictions of George Fox and the early Quakers. For a long time, Russell read the Bible every day, and he still refers to it several times a week. He also finds inspiration in the poems of John Greenleaf Whittier, the Quaker poet. And for recreation, he is a fan of mystery writers and has a large collection of Agatha Christie and Sherlock Holmes.

Russell appreciates his childhood training by dedicated Sunday school teachers. One special teacher had the children memorize Bible verses and rewarded them with boat rides on the White River on Sunday afternoons. When inclement weather prevented these outings, the children played indoor games and enjoyed books in their meetinghouse, which was regularly open and available under adult supervision.

Before Russell's time the Paoli Friends had become a pastoral meeting, as many Friends meetings did during the evangelical revivals that took place in the Midwest in the 1870s. Although he grew up in a pastoral meeting, he feels at home in unprogrammed worship and says, "Organizational church is not as important as what you feel, as the things that come to you in times of meditation. The silence is significant and the understanding deeper than what is learned in Sunday school. At times in formal meetings, words are needed. I feel at home in both pastoral and nonpastoral meetings."

As a young man of draft age, Russell found his religious convictions put to severe test by the call to stop Adolf Hitler's insane genocide. "I had strong reservations," he said, "which were balanced by the dastardly nature of Hitler. At that young age, it seemed like the right thing to do." In World War II he was at first in the Fourth Armored Division at Pine Camp, New York, and then was assigned to the Tenth Armored Division at Fort Knox, Kentucky. He went with that division to Cherbourg, France. He and two other young men in that division were Quakers from Indiana. One day they got a call from the commander's office, where they were told that because of their religious background they were being transferred to the Medical Department. They were surprised because they had not been aware of this possibility. Russell returned home after nearly two years of service in Europe.

The need to be practical during a time of severe economic depression led Russell to give up his chosen study of geology at Indiana University after three years and enroll at the Utilities Engineering Institute in Chicago. He received a diploma from the institute and set up a heating, refrigeration, and air-conditioning business in his hometown of Paoli. Finally, a back problem forced him to give up the business in 1945. He moved to Bloomington, where he joined the Local of the Building Crafts Union and worked in maintenance at the Sarkes Tarzian company until his retirement.

Since transferring membership from Paoli Meeting to Bloomington, Russell has taken much of the responsibility of our meeting for sharing in the work of the parent body, Western Yearly Meeting. He is now in his second term as a member of the Board on Christian Ministries and Evangelism of Western Yearly Meeting. He was on the Executive committee for three years, and he served for a number of years as clerk of the Southern Area. He now heads the Long-Range Planning committee of our Bloomington meeting, and he has previously served on Ministry and Counsel and on the Maintenance committee.

Russell and Mary Jane (Hill) are the parents of four sons and two daughters, and the grandparents of six children. The couple were introduced by mutual friends in Indianapolis. Mary is also a birthright Quaker. She was born in Lawrence, Indiana, and brought up in California before returning to Indiana as a young adult.

Members and attenders in our Bloomington Friends Meeting come from a variety of backgrounds and from many places. We look to Friends Mary and Russell Comingore for support in maintaining continuity today with our Quaker heritage of more than three hundred years.

— Judy Edgerton, November 1990

QUAKER PROFILE No. 9:

Robert Schutt

A current idea from pop psychology is that the name of a person has an effect upon the developing personality. Robert Barclay Schutt was named Barclay after a great-uncle. All the same, the Robert Barclay who was the seventeenth-century Quaker comes to mind when one hears Rob Schutt's name.

With the longer name shortened to Rob, the twentieth-century Quaker namesake made clear in his teen years that he was going to go his own way insofar as religion was concerned. Past his junior high school age, Rob's parents, Walter and Dorothy Gilbert Schutt, did not insist that he attend Quaker functions. It was his choice not to do so, then and throughout his years as a student at Earlham College. Even his choice of a college was a rebellious one. Since Rob wanted to be different from his brother and two sisters, all of whom had gone to Earlham, he enrolled at the University of Rochester, expecting to major in astrophysics. That choice lasted for one semester, when a case of homesickness and a desire to change his course of study brought him to Earlham after all. There he majored in math because he was good at it, and also in English because he loved it.

The questioning teenager has now become the mature, seeking Quaker that we know as clerk of Bloomington Friends Meeting. Rob gives credit to his parents for an upbringing in which the family custom was attendance at Sunday school and church services, but without a feeling of pressure. His adult religious experience he describes as one of "perpetual discovery." He says: "I have struggled with certain aspects of Quakerism all my life, but my commitment to Quakerism in general and to our Bloomington meeting in particular grows stronger each day." He mentions Thomas Kelly's *Testament of Devotion* as having had a profound influence on his religious life.

Rob speaks of one person in particular as being influential in his return to an interest in Quakerism. It is Lorton Heusel, who was a young pastor in the Wilmington (Ohio) Friends Meeting where the Schutt family were members as Rob was growing up. When Rob began his career as a math teacher at Hamilton Heights High School, just north of Indianapolis, he and his wife Amy joined First Friends Meeting, where Lorton Heusel is now pastor. He had dedicated Rob as a baby in the Wilmington meeting. "I have known him all my life," Rob said. "He also dedicated [son] Tom in Indianapolis." Then Rob added, "He can inspire on a weekly basis."

Asked whether his religious convictions influence him in his association with the students he now teaches in English and math classes at Brown County High School, Rob answered that he believes he "unconsciously teaches in a Quakerly way." He stressed participation in his classes because "I don't like people sitting and not participating. Unprogrammed Friends believe that. Earlham strengthened that." He especially enjoys a course in Russian literature, which he teaches in English. The class was developed by Rob at the high school and draws good students. "There are universal truths in literature," he says. "On the surface, people are different, but the more you study and read, the more similarities there are."

Rob takes pride in his parents' leadership roles in the Society of Friends. Dorothy Schutt came from the Church of the Brethren, another peace church, and Walter Schutt had been brought up as a Methodist before they both became Quakers. Both parents "have always been active with Wilmington Friends Meeting and in Wilmington Yearly Meeting," Rob says. His father, Attorney Walter Schutt, was presiding clerk of Friends United Meeting for three years and of the Friends Committee on National Legislation in Washington, D.C. for a number of years. He is well remembered by those who attended the Bloomington Friends' fall retreat in 1989 as a dynamic discussion leader.

Rob spoke warmly of his three siblings, saying, "We are a close family." One sister, Elizabeth, shares his love of teaching, after having served in the Peace Corps in Zaire. Family signatures appear on the wedding certificate, along with signatures of all other relatives and friends who were in attendance at the traditional Quaker wedding when Robert Barclay Schutt and Amy Claire Slotten were married in her home town of Carlisle, Pennsylvania. Amy and Rob had met in a class in English Romanticism as students at Earlham. Their framed wedding certificate hangs on the wall of their Bloomington home.

Rob and Amy first came to Bloomington in 1983 and later transferred their membership from the Indianapolis Friends meeting to ours in Bloomington. Their four-year-old son, Thomas Harlan Schutt, was born in Bloomington. They have attended Bloomington Friends Meeting regularly during the past five years, taking on increasingly more responsibility for the meeting. Rob's service as clerk of the meeting and Amy's clerkship of the Education committee are vital to the life of our meeting.

— Judy Edgerton, December 1990

QUAKER PROFILE No. 10:

William Z. Shetter

For anyone wishing to meet a truly convinced Friend, solidly placed in the Quaker way of life, William Zeiders Shetter is that Friend. Birthright Friends grow into the searching spirit that is the Quaker way. Convinced Friends find themselves in tune by way of a "convergence of ideas," a phrase Bill Shetter used in describing his early association with Radnor Friends Meeting in the Philadelphia area of Pennsylvania. He was a mature person, already well established in his academic profession, having just joined the faculty at Bryn Mawr College, when he and Janette Knott Shetter first attended Radnor Meeting in 1962. They had met as graduate students at the University of California (Berkeley), where Janette earned her Ph.D. in biochemistry and Bill earned his in German. Bill said the exploration of ideas that he and Janette had made for themselves as they were reading and searching seemed to match those they discovered in Quaker discussion groups. Membership was a natural transition because, he said, "we had matured enough to attach ourselves to a meeting." They came to Bloomington and our Friends meeting in 1965, with daughter Jessica and son Martin, then young children.

Bill was unaware of Quakers as he was growing up, "except as a part of history." In spite of the prominent role of William Penn and early Quakers in the history of Pennsylvania, visible religious sects in his hometown of Allentown were those of the original German settlers in that area of the state, among them the Mennonites. Bill's parents were Baptists and he grew up in that church, where his father was organist. His grandparents were Mennonites, with simplicity as their approach to living — an approach that Bill seems to have acquired naturally, and that made him feel at home with the emphasis on simplicity in the Philadelphia Yearly Meeting's book of discipline.

Bill's simplicity in manner and speech is evident in the direct, forthright approach to the task at hand as he continues to be active in our Friends meeting, in Western Yearly Meeting, and in the Friends World Committee for Consultation. He was clerk of our meeting for several years. He was also on Ministry and Counsel, and served on the Nominating committee, first as a member and then as clerk. He has worked with the Peace and Social Concerns committee and the Finance committee. He is currently serving with the latter and is clerk of the Burial Ground committee. He has been a representative of Western Yearly Meeting to the Friends World Committee (FWC) for three years. He is now clerk of the FWC subcommittee that is responsible for interpreting the aims and activities of that organization to the various branches of the Society of Friends. Bill's and Janette's association with the FWC has taken them to meetings in Des Moines, Iowa, and in Switzerland, Mexico, and Japan. The annual business meeting this year is to take place in March in Houston, Texas. Bill's facility with languages has stood him in good stead as he serves Western Yearly Meeting on this international committee. He was invited by Cuban Friends to visit and speak at several of their meetings in August 1986.

With so much energy and time spent in Quaker work, the word commitment comes to mind, which might be described as service grounded in a lifelong religious experience. Bill had what he describes as an "old-fashioned upbringing" by his Baptist parents, in which he memorized verses from the Bible in Sunday school and attended prayer meetings on Wednesday nights. He objected to this interviewer's reference to him as a student of the Bible, yet he has for a number of years taken a leading role in a Bible discussion group preceding our meeting for worship. He describes the Bible as an "important record of people's religious groping, a part of continuing revelation for all of us if we continue to work at it." He admittedly emphasizes the Bible more strongly than many Friends do, saying it is "continually fresh as revelation takes place for us." He believes Jesus was a real flesh-and-blood person with human failures, in spite of all the myths that have grown up around him. "The real person behind it all has relevance to modern life and means much more than the story of the Virgin Birth." He expresses himself as "sympathetic to the mystical tradition of Quakerism." He expresses optimism concerning the future of our Friends meeting, saying that it has definite strengths and he does not regard "bumps on the way as disastrous."

Bill's approach to students in the classroom reflects his Quaker philosophy. He "treats students the same as Meeting people," and he likes discussion and drawing them out rather than lecturing to them. Trying to bring out the best in his students is more important than "imparting knowledge." His title at Indiana University is Professor of Germanic Languages, and his classes are in Dutch language and culture and Germanic linguistics. The Dutch grammar compiled by Bill has become a standard work in America for students of that language. Altogether, his three books have now sold 100,000 copies. His most recent book, *The Netherlands in Perspective*, published in 1987, is an introduction to Dutch culture. Research in his field has required much time spent in the Netherlands since his first sojourn as a Fulbright Scholar. On September 17, 1985, he was decorated by the Dutch government, receiving a document, by order of the House of Orange, in the name of the Queen of the Netherlands. The ceremony took place in the Dutch embassy in Washington, and was attended by Senator J. William Fulbright.

The Shetters' home has always been open to Friends for group meetings as well as to individual Friends. They have also offered the hospitality of their home to Friends from other places in the United States and abroad. They have become contact persons for a number of people who have attended our meeting while in Bloomington and then left to follow careers elsewhere. Their telephone number is at the top of our newsletter for the convenience of those persons who need to be in touch with someone from the Meeting. An appropriate descriptive title for Bill and Janette — if Quakers awarded titles — might be Ambassadors for Bloomington Friends Meeting.

— Judy Edgerton, January 1991

QUAKER PROFILE No. 11:

Peter Burkholder

> We Quakers are concerned first with what we can experience, including divine revelation.
>
> — James Peter Burkholder

Thus Peter is placed in the tradition of the Quaker mystic. He experiences a strong sense of the Divine in worship, which is not present for him "in churches where a priest mediates. We are responsible for our own selves. Nothing is handed to us on a silver platter. I must be prepared — centered. I try to get myself into an attitude of worship. If I'm not profiting by the silence, I can't profit by the messages. I'm not waiting for someone else to do something for me." In the spirit of complete openness that characterized the interview for this profile, Peter continued: "I notice willfulness in myself. My favorite prayer is Jesus' prayer in the Garden of Gethsemane: 'Not my will, but Thine be done' — a prayer to serve God and lay aside my willfulness." He feels that Friends meeting for worship is hard work, and regrets that often he finds thoughts about work hindering his ability to become centered in worship. He "likes the spirit" in our own meeting for worship.

Peter's religious journey has been one of self-discovery in a family that was unchurched, although each parent came from a rich religious heritage. Peter had his first religious experience at the age of ten in a summer camp run by Quakers in the Pocono Mountains of Pennsylvania. On Sunday mornings the leader took his campers, who were of various religious faiths, to what Peter describes as a campfire circle, where they experienced silent worship, after some words which he does not remember. The silence for young Peter was a moving experience. Later in his senior year in high school, Mormon missionaries persuaded him to read their literature, thus stimulating questions and exploration beyond the literature into religious thinking on his own.

As a freshman at Earlham College (Richmond, Indiana), Peter felt at home immediately in Clear Creek Friends Meeting. He applied for membership the following year and became a member in 1973. He changed his membership to Urbana Friends Meeting (Illinois) while in graduate school at the University of Chicago, and then became a member of 57th Street Meeting in Chicago. He is now a member of Madison Friends Meeting (Wisconsin), to which he transferred after joining the University of Wisconsin faculty.

Peter's deep sense of the Divine was manifested in a mystical experience in his sophomore year at Earlham College, following a search for direction in his life. He had been uncertain about choosing a major course of study, logically concluding that the choice of a profession should dictate that decision. Quite suddenly, while walking across the campus, he had a revelation, which he describes as a sense of the Divine. It came as a message that said: "You are going to be a college professor. Now figure out what of." The choice was easy, for he had tried a course in political science and found it to be dull, while the class he took in music theory was enjoyable. He had played the clarinet since age nine, had sung in choirs in both grade school and high school, had studied voice, and had been assigned to leading roles in two Gilbert and Sullivan operettas. So now at Earlham College he was on his way, studying both voice and piano and singing in the two college choirs. His music education was completed at the University of Chicago, first with an M.A. in composition and musicology in 1980 and then with his Ph.D. in 1982 in musicology.

"Intellectual" can be added to our description of Peter as a mystic. As an educator, he is the norm rather than the exception in a family where his father and two uncles are college professors, a fourth uncle is a public school superintendent, and his mother is president of the school board in Urbana, Illinois. Jean Burkholder has used her skills and training, which include music and go beyond a college degree, to bring up Peter and his brother and sister in an atmosphere of social service. He attributes his ability to feel comfortable in the company of all kinds of people to his upbringing in Urbana, where his father is professor of mathematics at the University of Illinois, and in a home visited by people from many parts of the world.

Examining his own motivation, Peter wrestled with himself when he faced the question of the military draft and became a conscientious objector at age eighteen, the year after he joined the Society of Friends. The feeling of being different as a Quaker in the largely conformist world was similar to what he later encountered when he discovered that he was destined to live a different life from the majority of society: he realized that he is gay. It was comforting, he said, when he discovered Friends for Lesbian and Gay Concerns, made up of people who are both Quakers and gay or lesbian. He defines gay as a kind of spirit, not synonymous with homosexual. In a conformist society, his realization was "very scary," but he knew it was important to be open with his family and with Urbana Friends Meeting. His family came to be understanding and the meeting was very supportive.

Peter's father, Donald Lyman Burkholder, is from a family of Mennonites who emigrated from Switzerland in the 1740s to Lancaster County, Pennsylvania. He was a conscientious objector in World War II, assigned to hospital and ambulance work in New Jersey. He too is a graduate of Earlham College, where he met Jean Annette Fox, whom he married. Great-grandfather Peter Burkholder joined the Church of the Brethren after marrying someone of that faith, and moved to rural Nebraska, where Peter's grandfather and father grew up. Peter's mother, Jean Fox Burkholder, is of British ancestry. Her father was a diplomat in the British consulate in Philadelphia in the early 1900s. The family tree included Quakers, among them such well-known personalities as Carolyn Fox, Joseph John Gurney, and Elizabeth (Gurney) Fry. It is interesting to note that Earlham College got its name from the Gurney estate.

A brief summary of Peter's academic achievements includes membership on the faculty at the University of Wisconsin from 1982 to 1988 and his present associate professorship here at Indiana University in the School of Music, where he teaches courses and seminars in music history. He publishes in journals in his field and has authored a prize-winning book: *Charles Ives: The Ideas Behind the Music* (Yale University Press, 1985). He likes writing and requires it of his students, including term papers and the keeping of journals. Friends are the beneficiaries of Peter's concise and accurate minutes as recording clerk of Bloomington Meeting. He had articles published in *Friends Journal* in 1983, in the May first and the November first issues. We wish we could reprint both in toto, especially the second — a deeply moving tribute to his beloved sister Kathy, who died quite suddenly at age twenty-eight. A quotation from that article seems appropriate for all of us at this trying time in our national history:

> We cannot demand of ourselves or of other people that we save the world. That is not what God calls us to do. However inadequate we feel, if we are bending our ways to the leadings of the Spirit, in our work, and in our relationships, if we serve life even for the briefest moment, we are a cause for God's rejoicing.

— Judy Edgerton, February 1991

QUAKER PROFILE No. 12:

Ruth Jones Wentworth

Born into a Quaker family and educated from first grade until college entrance in Friends schools, Ruth Jones Wentworth takes for granted a serene life of service. She feels no need to read Quaker history and literature; she is both a part of living Quaker tradition and a product of it. "I have always taken Quaker meeting for worship for granted as part of my life," she says.

We are privileged to draw upon a chronological documentation of the main events in Ruth's life that she prepared for our interview, beginning with her birth in Lansdowne (near Philadelphia), the daughter of Samuel W. and Florence M. Jones. Her parents and her older brother and sister are now deceased.

Ruth describes her growing-up years as simple, her family as quiet and considerate of one another. The family routinely attended Lansdowne Friends Meeting on Sundays, after Ruth's father had read aloud to them from the Bible. Her parents sat on the raised facing benches, and she sat in the back with the other children. Her memory of First-day school is that the children sang and there was a collection of pennies.

Ruth's first six years of schooling were at Lansdowne Friends School, her next three at Friends Select in Philadelphia, and she is a graduate of Westtown School, Westtown, Pennsylvania. Her leadership was recognized during her senior year at Westtown when she was elected president of the girls' student body. The school was coeducational, but in the 1920s and 1930s strict separation of the sexes extended to boys and girls being seated on opposite sides of the room during meeting for worship, held at midweek as well as on First-days. The school maintained a religious atmosphere, emphasizing religious studies and requiring the memorization of Bible verses, one to be recited each week and the whole collection periodically.

The school's requirement for participation in sports was not a hardship for the outdoors-loving and athletically inclined Ruth. She had enjoyed living in a somewhat rural setting at home in Lansdowne, which has since become a more heavily populated suburb. She recalls her childish embarrassment when she was late one day at grade school because the family dog had followed her and she had to take it home. She says perhaps that is why she has felt impelled to be on time everywhere ever since!

Ruth learned to play basketball at Friends Select School and added field hockey and tennis at Westtown. She followed her mother's advice to major in physical education at Connecticut College for Women and made it her profession, beginning with a year of teaching as an intern at Germantown Friends School. She then joined the teaching staff at Westtown School, where she served for two years. During a summer of graduate study at the University of Wisconsin at Madison, Ruth Jones met William Norris Wentworth, who was on the staff of the university. They were married during the Christmas holidays in 1936 under the care of Lansdowne Friends Meeting. Ruth resigned her faculty position at Westtown School the following June.

Ruth and Norris's first home was in Madison, Wisconsin. In 1941 they moved to Champaign, Illinois. Then they lived for a brief period in Oak Ridge, Tennessee, just before coming to Bloomington in the fall of 1945. During the growing-up years of their two children, Nancy and Samuel, Ruth's life was one of service to her family and the community. Ruth's teaching experience, her love of the outdoors, her unusual energy (she has always slept only four or five hours each night), and her organizational skills made her an ideal leader when scouting for girls was developing in Bloomington. She was involved in this work from 1947 to 1967, as the leader of several different troops. She was sent to the national Girl

Scouts training camp in New York State; afterwards she trained leaders here in Bloomington, becoming chairman of the local training committee. As such, she was a board member of the Girl Scout Council. She enlisted husband Norris's help as co-chairman with her of the Girl Scout camp at Bradford Woods, just north of Bloomington. Together Ruth and Norris laid out the camp and developed the troop cabin.

Ruth's energies turned to a new career in 1961 when she was placed in charge of filing at the catalog department of the Indiana University Library. She held that position until her retirement ten years later, when Norris retired from his work as director of the University Conference Bureau.

Meanwhile, both Nancy and Sam had graduated from the Indiana University Medical School and were following careers in medicine: Nancy took a doctorate in nursing and Sam an M.D. specializing in children's diabetes. Nancy is married to Robert Dolphin, university professor and administrator, and lives in Durango, Colorado. Sam is married to Sondra Callahan Wentworth, registered nurse, and lives in Danville, Indiana. Ruth's skills and capacity for organization were then put to use as a volunteer at Opportunity House, a used-clothing outlet, the proceeds of which go to the support of Monroe County United Ministries (formerly known as the Christian Center), a kind of settlement house serving low-income and destitute people of all ages, and including a preschool daycare center. In 1982–83 Ruth chaired a committee to make an addition to Opportunity House and enlarge the store. At the present time she spends part of each week working as a volunteer at the House.

In recognition of her service in scouting, Ruth was honored at a special ceremony in 1966 with the award of a pin and a Girl Scout statuette. She was recognized by the Bloomington Exchange Club in May 1986 for her "outstanding community service to Bloomington and Monroe County" and was awarded a plaque on which was inscribed "The Book of Golden Deeds."

In addition to her work as a homemaker and community leader Ruth has devoted time to our Friends meeting, from its beginning in 1950 down to the present. Her calm demeanor and natural Quakerly approach to all facets of Bloomington

Meeting continue to provide a stabilizing influence in our diverse and ever-shifting Meeting population. Her orderly habits and dedication to any job she undertakes make her the ideal person to keep the membership records of the meeting. In addition, she has served as recording clerk, taught First-day school, and served on various committees. She takes responsibility for this work at the present time as a member of the Maintenance committee. She and Norris have always extended the hospitality of their home both to individuals and for committee meetings. She is unusually sensitive to the needs of members and attenders, going out of her way to help people who have real problems or simply to take food and good cheer to people who are ill. Ruth is truly one of the foundation stones upon which our Bloomington Friends Meeting was built and still rests.

— Judy Edgerton, March 1991

QUAKER PROFILE No. 13:

Janette Knott Shetter

Intimations of the adult Janette Knott Shetter were there from her childhood. Born of two nature-loving scientists and living in a valley looking up at the Santa Lucia Mountains just sixteen miles from the Pacific Ocean, the little girl became a woman in the forefront of those who, late in our century, are working to save the environment. She says, "The quiet of the hikes in those mountains was a time for being at one with nature and reaching beyond oneself." In a Pendle Hill pamphlet she wrote, *Rhythms of the Ecosystem*, Janette says: "Man is only just beginning to become aware of the destructive effects he can have upon the earth." The pamphlet is in our Friends meeting library. It is a profound discourse that draws upon both religious and scientific knowledge to place mankind in God's eternal plan.

Janette grew up in what she describes as a liberal Methodist church, the only child of Charles Elgin Knott and Pearl Pemberton Knott, in the historic mission town of San Luis Obispo, California. Her father taught electrical engineering in an industrial school, and her mother had been a chemistry and home-economics teacher. "There was never any doubt that I would become a scientist," Janette said. Her mother made certain that she should have her first course in biology as early as the eighth grade. The young adult Janette earned a doctorate in biochemistry at the University of California at Berkeley.

Janette began her independent religious searching as an undergraduate by visiting various churches, among them a

Friends meeting which she attended briefly. She also took part in an American Friends Service Committee weekend work camp in the inner city of San Francisco. Meanwhile, in another church, a study group exploring the Hindu *Bhagavad-Gita* attracted her attention. It was there that she met William Zeiders Shetter, a graduate student of German at Berkeley. They were married on September 12, 1953. Bill had grown up as a Baptist, but was singing in a Methodist church choir. They became members of Radnor Friends Meeting in 1962 after moving to Rosemont, Pennsylvania, near Bryn Mawr College, where Bill was teaching.

Janette describes her first fifteen minutes in meeting for worship at the Radnor meeting as "something that is hard to put into words, but it is the feeling you get of coming home." Radnor Meeting member Dorothy Steere was her role model. "In her quiet way," she said, "through informal reading and discussion groups in her home, she taught me what Friends are all about." Other Friends whom Janette mentions as significant along her religious journey are Carolyn Kellum, who was a member of Indiana Conservative Yearly Meeting in Plainfield from whom she first learned about the Friends World Committee for Consultation, and Helen Hole, a member of Clear Creek Friends Meeting in Richmond, Indiana, whom Janette values for her insight into the qualities and necessary ingredients for "the gathered meeting." She was also influenced by Evelyn Underhill's *Mysticism*, the classic work on the medieval mystics.

Meditation is undoubtedly the source of the energy Janette devotes to the Society of Friends, using the network already in place to work with the Society for the creation of a better world. In her meditation she has "experienced strong leadings." Some of them, which came to her in situations of extreme anxiety, she regards as genuinely mystical experiences. She employs a single focus in her daily meditation, sometimes reading passages from devotional literature. She finds her private meditation to be helpful preparation for centering down in meeting for worship on Sundays. "We make contact with something beyond ourselves. There is grace — acceptance and grace — a marvelous combination that is a gift from God in the silence with other Friends."

Janette and Bill and their young children, Jessica and Martin, came to Bloomington when Bill joined the Indiana University faculty in 1965. In contacts with longtime Friends and newcomers alike in our meeting, Janette's enthusiasm is contagious as she looks for ways to bring out the best in each individual. She is sensitive to the human network of community in the meeting. Quoting from George Fox in his journal, Janette says: "I think of his words as an ideal for our own Friends meeting — to see that of God in all those who come to us."

Janette's responsibilities have included the committee on Ministry and Counsel, on which she recently served as clerk for two terms in succession. She is currently on the Peace and Social Concerns and Friends on Campus committees. She meets with a worship-sharing group on a weekly basis.

This past July 1990, our meeting was represented by Janette as she worked with a Western Yearly Meeting committee in planning for the Friends United Meeting Triennial, held on the Indiana University campus and attended by delegates from six countries and thirteen yearly meetings. She and other volunteers from our meeting were at the Triennial throughout its session, working in various capacities, including taking part in programming.

Janette believes there is a natural relation between Friends' spirituality and concern for the environment. In connection with the Triennial she brought her environmental concerns to the attention of the appropriate committees, leading them to arrange for less air conditioning in the dormitories and for recycling all the various kinds of discarded paper. She endorses the request by the Friends Committee on Unity with Nature to have a query on the environment included in all books of discipline for use by monthly meetings. While remaining centered, she is at the same time mindful of "interrelatedness as expressed in such things as the human-potential and feminist movements, in New Age thinking, and in environmental concerns — all of which represent a different way of looking at things."

Janette serves on the Western Yearly Meeting administrative council, which meets twice each year to carry on business when the Yearly Meeting is not in session; she has recently been appointed to the Board on Peace and Christian Social Concerns. She has represented WYM on the personnel committee of the Friends World Committee for six years, four of them as clerk. She values that experience, and says, "I learned how Friends succeed in getting the best from people." In March of this year she was an observer for WYM at a meeting of the Friends Committee on Unity with Nature, which took place in Houston, Texas, at the same time and place as the annual meeting of the Friends World Committee's Section of the Americas, to which Bill Shetter is the delegate from WYM.

Janette's leadership abilities have been recognized by Pendle Hill (the Friends study and conference center located near Philadelphia), where she is serving on the Executive Board. Her first experience at Pendle Hill came in 1971 when she and her family spent a semester there as residents and students while she taught a course in ecology. She says that was a transition period for her, "a valuable growing experience where I learned new ways of thinking about myself and about living with other people." *Rhythms of the Ecosystem* grew out of the course she taught.

Although Janette has used her academic training in the undergraduate classrooms of three institutions, her skills, religious insight, and incredible energies have been concentrated over the years on human needs in her own family and in the family of Friends wherever she has found them. A goal that the Friends World Committee has set for itself is one that Janette would like to see adopted as a challenge in our Bloomington Meeting's relations with Western Yearly Meeting. It reads as follows: "To facilitate loving understanding of diversities among Friends while we discover together, with God's help, our own common spiritual ground."

—Judy Edgerton, April 1991

QUAKER PROFILE No. 14:

Howard Haines Turner

A ready smile and a soft-spoken, easy manner belie a determination and a faith that moves mountains. That describes Howard Haines Turner, born of Quaker parents in Brooklyn, New York, and educated from kindergarten through college entirely in Quaker schools. He says that it was a sheltered life, in which he went to Friends meeting and First-day school with the same young people he saw every day in Brooklyn Friends School. Opportunity for broader acquaintance came when he took an extra year at George School, Pennsylvania, before entering Swarthmore College. During vacations at Buck Hill Falls, a Quaker resort in the Pocono Mountains, he became friends with a young girl named Catherine Pierson — she was 12 and he was 13 when they met — and eight years later they were married.

During those growing-up years Haines liked getting out of the city and working with the hired man who looked after a forty-acre farm belonging to the Turners. The difference between a way of life where people lived by manual labor and the way of life of his father's wealthy business associates, whom he got to know when he spent time with them as a golf caddie, made a profound and lasting impression on Haines. He liked working with humbler people and he developed a sense of equality that made him feel there was "no justification for riches and privilege."

Haines's family consisted of three brothers and a sister, an aunt who lived with them, and his mother and father, whom he speaks of as loving parents. His mother's name was Charlotte Chapman Turner. He was named for his maternal grandfather, Noah Haines Chapman. His maternal grandmother, Mariana Wright Chapman, was an activist in the women's suffrage movement in the late 1800s and was president of its New York State Society for Women's Suffrage for six years. The Chapmans were originally from Ohio. The family of Henry Chandlee Turner, Haines's father, came from Maryland's Eastern Shore. Henry Turner was a successful businessman, the founder of the Turner Construction Company, which pioneered the development of reinforced concrete. A plaque by the steps of the Columbia University subway entrance in New York City records that it was built in 1905 by the Turner Construction Company.

Haines's early identification with a more basic way of life than what seemed possible in the business world merged with ideals he absorbed while growing up in Quaker schools, and was reinforced during his years at Swarthmore. It matured into important choices he was to make later. Haines calls himself a rebel. Courses in labor problems as a part of his preparation for a Ph.D. in economics at Columbia University helped to clarify his direction in what he terms his antibusiness philosophy. He wrote a letter to his father telling him that he did not believe in inheritance and returned the stocks and bonds that had already been given to him. He was unable to rescind a trust fund in his name, however, and he uses the income from that mainly for philanthropic causes. He says of his father, "He was encouraging and forgiving, and always interested in what I was doing."

The political ideals of the well-known Socialist Norman Thomas were closer to Haines's outlook at the time he was a graduate student than those of either major political party. His first job after passing the qualifying examinations for the doctorate in 1933 was as a statistician with the economic adviser to President Franklin D. Roosevelt and his cabinet. He left the job in order to study the cooperative movement in Massachusetts and Minnesota. This led to his appointment as education secretary for the District of Columbia Cooperative Federation. That experience furnished material for his doctoral dissertation, "Case Studies of Consumer Cooperatives," completed in 1941. In that same year, Haines was appointed to the staff of Pendle Hill, the Quaker center for religious and social study at Wallingford, Pennsylvania.

He has taught college and university undergraduates at various times and felt dissatisfied. "I believed in adult education. Pendle Hill gave me that opportunity," he said. Adult education has now become a priority in universities and colleges, but Haines was prepared by training and experience to do early innovative work in that field at Pendle Hill. From 1941 to 1944 he led students who were often older than college age to do field work helping people in the Chester area near Philadelphia. Then in 1945 he took on the challenging assignment of educating people in the labor unions. He not only taught them economics but organized weekend conferences at Pendle Hill and brought in specialists on topics of interest to working people. He broadened their outlook by providing them with experiences as simple as taking part with student crews in meal preparation and dish-washing, attending the half-hour morning meetings for worship, or — in response to one union's request — learning about the trees and flowers on the grounds at Pendle Hill. "The time spent at Pendle Hill with Howard and Anna Brinton was a major influence in my life," he said. Howard Brinton was Director of Studies, and Anna Brinton's title was Administrative Director.

Haines took a leave of absence from Pendle Hill to learn firsthand about working as a laborer. He and Catherine (Cay) and their three young sons — 14-year-old Clark, 9-year-old Richard, and 7-year-old Rigbie — drove a Ford station wagon with a tent-trailer to Washington State, Arizona, and Indiana, while Haines worked in an orchard, on a surveyor's crew, on a production line in a Chevrolet factory, and on a livestock farm.

In 1957 Haines joined the faculty of Earlham College in Richmond, Indiana. He moved from there to Indiana University and hence to our Friends meeting in 1959. As Associate Professor of Labor Education and Research, Haines set up committees of labor union officers, organized conferences and classes, and selected teachers for centers across the state. He also led a study tour to Europe in 1973 and set up another tour in 1977. He found the work to be "very rewarding, because there was a great need for this kind of help, and people were interested and appreciative." Haines's pioneering work in this field prepared the way in the School of Continuing Studies for the present Division of Labor Studies, which now has sixteen members. Haines retired from Indiana University in 1978.

Haines declared himself a pacifist as a result of the Selective Service Act of 1940, but was never drafted. When the United States declared war on North Vietnam in 1965, he got in touch with the American Friends Service Committee, volunteering to be of service in helping victims of the war. He was sent to South Vietnam in 1966 under the AFSC's Volunteers for International Service Project to set up a program in which four American pacifists assisted native Vietnamese social agencies. During eight months after his return to Philadelphia in 1967 he also recruited medical staff for a clinic at a civilian hospital in central Vietnam, where work with amputees was one of the greatest needs. There American and British specialists trained a staff of forty-five Vietnamese, who continued the work after the northern armies took control.

In 1975 Haines helped with the financing of Harmony School in Bloomington, founded in order to serve children from low-income, broken homes. The school has now become a thriving alternative school, with 180 students from elementary through high school, attracting families dissatisfied with our public schools as well as low-income families. Haines remains on the advisory board of the school and helps in the solicitation of funds.

"I'm still a rebel," Haines said as he talked about Citizens for Jail Improvement, which he and other concerned people organized here in Bloomington in 1980. A more recent addition is Juvenile Justice. Both groups could be considered citizens functioning as watchdog organizations, to make conditions of incarceration as humane as possible. At this writing, Haines is joined by Elizabeth Buck and Paddy Reid from our meeting in visiting the inmates at the Monroe County jail on Tuesday evenings. Haines spends many hours in follow-up in a spirit of friendship for some of the young offenders after they have been released.

The Community Kitchen, serving meals to hungry people, was started in 1982 with the help of both Haines and Cay Turner, who advised and assisted in the implementation of the program until it was well established.

At the present time much of Haines's energy goes into the clerkship of the committee on Ministry and Counsel of our Friends meeting. He is known to work quietly with individuals who are in some difficult situation. Except on occasions when he is out of town, he regularly attends meeting for worship on Sundays, adding to the spirit of the meeting by his presence and by his spoken messages. Haines's own term "rebel" is the driving force behind a faith that moves mountains.

— Judy Edgerton, May 1991

PROFILE No. 15:

Elizabeth Louise Koop Buck

Elizabeth Koop Buck's first experience in a Friends meeting was here in Bloomington. "I was overcome by the silence in my first meeting for worship," she said. "This was heaven-sent, so much so that at first I resented people speaking. I felt it was a wonderful time to think my own thoughts without interruption."

Elizabeth (Lib) is trained in philosophy. Her approach to Quakerism is that of a philosopher and intellectual, but with a deep empathy with other human beings. One thing that attracted her to Quakerism is a tolerance of different points of view. Her father, William Walter Koop, was a Catholic and a Democrat; her mother, Eleanor Anderson Koop, was a Congregationalist and a Republican. They agreed that any boys they had would be brought up as Catholics, and the girls as Congregationalists. Their three sons and two daughters each made their own choice as adults. One son is an atheist, another a Catholic, and the third a born-again Baptist. One daughter is a nun in the order of the Sisters of Loretto, and the other, our Lib Buck, is a Quaker. The tradition of pacifism in Lib's Quakerism coincides with her sister's activism as a pacifist. She not only runs a Catholic Worker home for transients in Denver, Colorado, but also demonstrates regularly at Rocky Flats, where the trigger mechanism for nuclear bombs is made.

The oldest in the family, Lib was born in Iowa City and grew up in Minnesota — mostly in Minneapolis. The tone of the Koop home was set by the loving spirit of Lib's father, whom she adored as everyone else did. He loved being with his family. "Once," says Lib, "when he was supposed to stay at home for a week after having a polyp removed, he stayed for a whole year." He was trained as a lawyer and had a successful practice in Minneapolis.

When Lib entered the University of Minnesota, she was a pre-med student. Later she gave that up and started accumulating credits for the sheer joy of learning, but without a defined major subject. She was graduated in six years instead of the usual four, with a liberal-arts degree. A professor of philosophy who was an acquaintance of hers steered her into that department for graduate work. She worked nights as a licensed x-ray technician at the university hospital and attended classes during the day.

Lib met Roger Conant Buck when they had desks in the same room where they were both teaching associates. They were married in 1948. In 1949 Roger won a Fulbright Grant for study at Oxford University, where they stayed for two years. The following year, Roger was assigned to teach at the University College of the Gold Coast in Ghana. Lib came home to Minneapolis before the year was out, preceding the birth of their daughter Lee. The baby was one week old when they moved to Chicago, where Roger joined the faculty of the University of Chicago in 1952. After one year there, the usual climb up the academic ladder led them around: three years at Duke University, a year at Ohio State University, and three years at Oberlin College, before settling permanently at Indiana University in 1960.

Lib's association with our Friends meeting was by a circuitous route. First we should say that Roger is "a third-generation atheist," who had little knowledge of the Bible. Since Lib and Roger realized that Western culture is based on the Bible, she gave him a Bible to read. She said he was amazed by what he discovered. They decided that their four children should learn about the Bible as part of their education, so they started reading it to them, beginning with the first chapter of Genesis. This was completely unsuccessful. Both Lib and Roger found some of the Old Testament accounts to be "horrifying." Lib then called several Bloomington churches to ask what they taught children in Sunday school. She got vague and unsatisfactory responses until she talked with Alice Leake of our Friends meeting, who told her that Quakers were teaching the

Bible. The Bucks enrolled their four children — Lee, Rocky, Wally, and Susan — in our First-day school. At first the children were dropped off by themselves, but they noticed that "other kids' families come with them."

In response to her children's request Lib began coming to our meeting. She had known some Quakers quite well, however, while still in college. They were conscientious objectors during World War II and were at the University of Minnesota serving as volunteer guinea pigs in a series of starvation experiments. She found these young men to be interesting company and dated some of them. Thus Quaker religious philosophy was not entirely new to her.

Lib said that she felt herself to be really a part of the Meeting when the clerk, who was JoAnna Henegar at the time, gave her a traveling minute to take to the Friends meeting at Oxford when Roger spent his sabbatical leave there in 1966–67. While they were there, Lee was enrolled at Sidcot, a Friends boarding school. During their later sojourns in England Susan also attended Sidcot. She liked it so much that after coming home she earned her own money with a paper route to pay for a return visit to her friends.

Lib transferred her membership from the Congregational church in Minneapolis to our Friends meeting. She now finds that she misses being at meeting when she is not able to attend. "So it is more than just a habit," she says. "I feel close to Meeting members and enjoy seeing the same people from week to week." She had not realized how complete her identification was until a good friend pointed out that she was answering questions about Quaker beliefs by saying "we believe" rather than "they believe." She has taught First-day school for a dozen years or so, and loves it. She has served on various committees, the latest being Ministry and Counsel.

During a series of discussions preceding meeting for worship in the mid-1970s, Monroe County Sheriff Bill Brown came one Sunday and talked about the situation at the jail. Lib's feeling of empathy at the description of the loneliness and neglect of the prisoners prompted her to present a daring scheme to the sheriff. She asked him to handcuff a prisoner to her and she would take that prisoner for a walk in the park.

The sheriff did not agree to that, but he did put her on a task force to examine jail problems.

Lib recalls that when she started visiting the jail, the first four visitors included a young conscientious objector to war who had been in prison, and his wife. They were soon joined in jail visitation by Haines Turner, of our meeting. Haines and the wife of the C.O. went to a Friends United Meeting workshop in Richmond, Indiana, dealing with the prison system and methods of improving it. Later, when jail visitation seemed in danger of being forbidden here, Lib and Haines assumed leadership in organizing Citizens for Jail Improvement so as to have stronger public support. The function of this organization continues to be the education of the public about jail conditions.

As we write this on Tuesday evening, Lib is at the jail talking with inmates. She is painfully aware of the misery of helpless people who are incarcerated, especially the poorest. She says her regular visits to talk with the prisoners at the county jail are a meaningful experience for her. "People are locked up not simply because of what they have done, but because they have no money for bail," she said. "We are warehousing the poor. There is minimal justice in our justice system." She is joined in these visits by Haines Turner and Paddy Reid from our meeting. She says that the present jail arrangement is less satisfactory than was the case in the previous jail facility. Arrangements are such that contacts are impossible with those who may need it the most, because people who are depressed remain in their cells and do not come out to see their visitors. Talking to the prisoners has become easier for her over time. Thus she gives what comfort she can to people who have been locked away from human contact.

In what seemed to be an expression of her hope for a better world, Lib said at the very end of our interview, "The most important thing is to give each child a head start by instilling pride in his [or her] own uniqueness."

— Judy Edgerton, June 1991

QUAKER PROFILE No. 16:

William Norris Wentworth

William Norris Wentworth will celebrate his ninetieth birthday next month, on August 21, 1991. We begin this profile by going back to the year 1913, when he was an impressionable twelve year old living with his family in State Center, Iowa. Responding to the usual emotional appeal of an evangelistic church service one Saturday night, he "went forward." But his independent thought overnight resulted in a different decision the next day. He told his mother that he was "not really excited by religion" and was not ready to join anything. He kept this resolve until his last year of high school at Tabor Academy (Tabor, Iowa), where he sang in the choir of the First Congregational Church, regularly attended by all the students. Although his degree at the University of Wisconsin in 1924 was from the College of Agriculture, his first job was as assistant pastor of Edwards Congregational Church in Davenport, Iowa. For five years after that, he was director of the Congregational Student Center at Iowa State College in Ames.

Norris is the seventh of eight children. His father traveled over the state of Iowa soliciting freight for transport to the eastern part of the country on the Star Union Line of the Pennsylvania Railroad. His father's work with the railroad kept him away from home as much as half of the year. Norris still has a wheelbarrow belonging to his father, symbolizing shared experiences of a close father-son relationship.

An indication of the religious atmosphere Norris grew up with can be seen in a piece of writing found among his

Presbyterian mother's papers after her death. It is titled "A Morning Resolve," which he describes as "a resolution to which she adhered as closely as a mortal could":

> I will try this day to live a simple, sincere, and serene life; repelling promptly every thought of discontent, anxiety, discouragement, impurity, and self-seeking; cultivating cheerfulness, magnanimity, charity, and the habit of holy silence; exercising economy in expenditure, carefulness in conversation, diligence in appointed service, fidelity in every trust, and a childlike trust in God.
>
> — John H. Vincent

Norris learned about Quakerism for the first time from Ruth Jones, a birthright Friend from Lansdowne, Pennsylvania, whom he met in 1935. She was a graduate student in summer school at the University of Wisconsin, and he was a member of the university staff for student counseling. They were married in 1936 under the care of Ruth's Meeting in Lansdowne. They lived in Wisconsin until 1940, when Norris accepted an appointment at the University of Illinois as director of Halls of Residence. After spending a year in Tennessee, where Norris was director of housing at the Manhattan Project, they settled down in Bloomington in 1945 when Norris joined the Indiana University staff as assistant director of residence halls. In 1950 he was appointed to set up a conference bureau for the university and remained its director for twenty-one years, until his retirement in 1971. His organizational skills and his genial manner undoubtedly gave a good first impression of the university to thousands of persons attending conferences here over the years.

It can be said of Norris that he is both gifted and innovative, with wide-ranging interests. His first love, he says, was agriculture, which he still prefers to other pursuits. A twice-daily chore, taking care of dairy cows, furnished him with practical experience while getting his B.A. degree in Genetics and Animal Husbandry at the University of Wisconsin. Lack of finances during the Great Depression kept him from completing graduate work toward an advanced degree in rural sociology. His natural talent for working with people has kept him in administrative positions throughout his career.

As a young boy still at home, he picked up a little knowledge of music just by observing an older sister, Lois, practice the piano. The boy would not have dreamed that as an adult, while working full time as head counselor in the residence halls at the University of Wisconsin, he would build on this scanty foundation to become a carillonneur. First, he was made chairman of a program to supervise the selection and installation of the carillon tower and bells. Then a carillonneur gave him a few concentrated lessons, and he was launched on his career as a carillon player — or, as he modestly puts it, a plain "bell ringer." For four years, from 1937 till 1941, he played the bells at eight in the morning, Monday through Friday, and in the evenings on Sunday. To this day he has a slightly bent finger which he says he got from pounding the bell keyboard.

Here in Bloomington and Monroe County, Norris is well-known in political circles for his many years of work as judge at one of the polling places. His responsibilities involved making sure an hour in advance of the opening that all was in order, overseeing a crew of eight persons, including a deputy sheriff, and then, after closing the poll, taking accurate official records to City Hall.

Those who have heard him open a polling place in his resonant baritone, calling "Hear ye, Hear ye!" at the door at 6 a.m., are not surprised to hear of his success as an announcer each fall for forty-five years, from 1930 to 1975, at the International Livestock Show in Chicago. He used a public address system in an amphitheater seating ten thousand people. It was his job to keep track of the ranking of animals by classes. At 7:30 in the morning he warned of judging to begin at 8:00, and evenings he was on duty for judging at the horse shows until 11 o'clock.

As soon as they had moved to Bloomington, Ruth and Norris got together with a few Quakers and started holding meetings for worship in each other's homes. Norris officially became a member of the Society of Friends as our meeting was being organized. The same freedom to think for himself that was important to the twelve-year-old boy remained important for the mature man, a freedom he recognized in a Quakerism free of hierarchy.

Bloomington Meeting began as a preparative meeting under the care of Blue River Monthly Meeting, and it enjoyed steady support from Western Yearly Meeting. Six adults and four children comprised the charter membership in 1950. Their first meeting place outside the homes of the members was the Bryan Room in the tower of the Indiana University Memorial Union. Norris took major responsibility, along with Ruth, Hazel Smith, Catherine Evans, and the late Keogh and Fay Rash. As the years passed, the meeting welcomed other Quakers to Bloomington and other seekers into full membership. In 1968 the firmly established Bloomington Friends Meeting acquired its own meetinghouse.

In addition to his organizing ability, Norris's interest in scholarship and history led him early on to begin his search into Quaker history and philosophy. He read widely in Quaker literature and says he depends on the writings of Howard Brinton for the fundamentals of Quakerism and on Rufus Jones as the interpreter. He appreciates Leonard Kenworthy's recent book entitled *Quakerism: A Study Guide* and articles by other Quakers in *Friends Journal.*

In his contacts with other meetings, Norris observed that the heart of an unprogrammed meeting is its library. He began collecting books, contributing a sizable number of them out of his own private collection, to form a library for the meeting. He obtained the advice of a trained librarian in setting up a system of cataloging. Single-handedly, he set about the work of cataloging a useful core of reference books and working with the late William Dietz to get the shelves we now see in the meetinghouse. He has been careful to preserve the collection of rare Quaker books that came from the Chapman-Turner family and from Pendle Hill, all of them dating before the turn of the century.

Norris acknowledges that his own well-documented family tree, traced back to colonial New England and even further back to England before the 1600s, has had much to do with his interest in the preservation of historic sites and genealogical records in Bloomington and Monroe County. As background for this profile, we were privileged to use the handsomely bound and amazingly complete Wentworth Family Tree. There is a Wentworth signature on the English Magna Carta, the charter of liberties to which the English barons forced King John to give his assent in 1215. A direct ancestor and one of the first English colonists in the New World, William Wentworth, signed the Plymouth Charter dated 1639. Norris's father, Elmer Marston Wentworth, was born in Newfield, Maine. His mother, Sarah Elizabeth Tilton Towne Wentworth, was born in Peabody, Massachusetts. Her family tree is included in the genealogy book and also extends back to the 1600s in England. Norris's four oldest siblings were born in New England, he and three others in the Midwest. Norris and Ruth's children, Nancy Wentworth Dolphin, D.N.S., of Durango, Colorado, and Samuel Wentworth, M.D., of Danville, Indiana, insure continuity of the family line.

Bloomington and Monroe County are indebted to Norris's work as a volunteer for much of the recent interest and accomplishment in the preservation of the history of the region. As president of the Monroe County Historical Society and chairman of the Old Library committee, he headed the group of citizens who saved the library building from destruction by a former mayor and others who wanted to make room for a parking lot. He has recently spent many hours in the archives of the county library working to preserve the genealogical records in more usable form.

One of Norris's earlier community-wide services was his cooperation with ministers of area churches who gave morning devotions on the local AM radio station. During the ten-minute period when Norris took his turn representing the Society of Friends, he read from the Bible or other devotional literature, giving quotations from Quaker sources along with his own comments. Appropriately, he has sometimes been referred to in the community as "Mr. Quaker."

It goes without saying that Norris has worked closely over the years with Blue River Quarterly Meeting and Western Yearly Meeting, including service on the board of the retirement home. He also served for a number of years until the age of retirement as a member of the board of trustees of Earlham College.

His life of service is firmly grounded in worship and awareness of a Supreme Being. He respects approaches to religion that are different from the Judeo-Christian concept. "I base my belief on how a religion affects the individual," he says. "There is not a God sitting there telling you what to do, but rather a Supreme Being on which you base your attitudes and standards of conduct. I am more interested in being helpful to society than in being ritualistic."

Norris has committed to memory favorite verses and passages from prose literature, saying: "They have 'spoken to my condition' in many ways. A few I may recite too often in meeting for worship, but they come to mind in my feeling of the Presence." We have found his quiet recitation of the following to be deeply moving:

> O Lord, support us all the day long, until the shadows lengthen and the evening comes, and the busy world is hushed, and the fever of life is over, and our work is done. Then in Thy mercy grant us a safe lodging and a holy rest, and peace at the last.
>
> — Sixteenth-century prayer
> from the Episcopal Book of Common Prayer

— Judy Edgerton, July 1991

QUAKER PROFILE No. 17:

Melanie Kell Isaacson

Historically, members of the Society of Friends have thought of themselves as a body of "seekers." Most Quakers believe in continuing revelation. The newest member of Bloomington Friends Meeting, Melanie Kell Isaacson, is in that tradition.

Melanie is not quite a native Bloomingtonian, although she spent a number of summers here as a child while her parents did graduate work at Indiana University. Then Melanie herself received her bachelor's degree from the university. She and her husband, Eric John Isaacson, met as students when they were freshmen and were married between their junior and senior years.

Now, twenty-two years later, they are back in Bloomington, together with their young daughter Erica. Eric, a computer specialist, has his own independent business as a software author. Melanie is busy with art work and other interests, not the least of which is our Friends meeting.

Melanie grew up in Evansville, Indiana, with an older sister Karen and a younger brother Bruce. Melanie's father, Henry Edward Kell, taught history in high school before retirement. Her mother, Ruth Aiken Kell, taught English. Both remain active in church and community affairs. Life in the Kell family was centered around Saint Paul's Episcopal Church, which Melanie describes as a fine old church situated near the Ohio River. Melanie's brother has his construction business here in Bloomington. Evansville is near enough that Melanie can see her parents and sister often. It is a pleasure to welcome Ruth and Henry Kell to meeting when they come to visit their daughter and her family.

Sometime during her undergraduate years, Melanie lost interest in church and felt comfortable being an agnostic. During her busy years as a doctoral candidate at Stanford University in California, she had no thought of any change in that decision. Yet, quite unexpectedly, her work in medieval literature, leading to her Ph.D. degree, played an important role in her evolving view of life and her own place in the world of the spirit.

After several more years in California at Silicon Valley in the San José area, she and Eric moved to Princeton, New Jersey, where Melanie worked for two years as a librarian at Princeton University while Eric was launching his career. Following the birth of their daughter, she said a growing feeling of dissatisfaction with her agnostic stance took hold of her. The responsibility for the new life in their home meant that Melanie was alone with the baby much of the time. This forced her back on her own resources without distractions, especially in the quiet of natural outdoor settings. Almost to her own surprise, she began to express herself in painting, as she still does today, ten years later. "Sitting alone in a field, intent on capturing the light, I found my agnosticism more uncomfortable," she said. "It was like meditation, or like a prayer. But I was disorganized, dissatisfied. Other people seemed to have found some direction. I was a late bloomer."

As an artist Melanie is drawn to the illuminating art done on ancient manuscripts, finding these an inspiration as she studies medieval literature and the lives of the saints. She identifies with the visionary material in these writings, which she has studied in depth. Both the theme of the search for the Holy Grail, first used in *Perceval* by the twelfth-century French poet Chrétien de Troyes, and all of Dante Alighieri's great fourteenth-century Christian poem *The Divine Comedy* have profound meaning for Melanie. She feels she has "wandered through dark woods, making wrong choices" — an identification with Dante himself in the first canto — and, "although it is never spelled out, there is an experience of the divine presence, a symbol of Christ's presence, in the Grail legend." In them both there is a depiction of spiritual crisis and growing awareness through trial and error.

Before exploring Friends Meeting, Melanie said she had only a vague idea about Quakerism beyond the impression that it was service-oriented. She had been looking at different churches but was uncomfortable with the dogma found in some. She could not imagine repeating words in church services that she could not personally believe. She thought briefly of Unitarianism, then wandered into our Friends meeting to see what it was like. From what she knew, she thought it might be demanding. "But," she added, "as other people have said of their first silent meeting for worship, the moment I walked in, it felt like home." She recalls what was said in meeting for worship that day because there was only one short message, spoken at the very end by Haines Turner: "And the power of the Lord was over all."

Melanie had entered fully into the life of the Meeting even before she became a member in February 1991. She says she enjoys the seriousness of Quaker group discussions and appreciates the religious orientation. She finds these sessions to be worthwhile, in contrast to those that go on in a secular setting or those that are simply materialistic in content. She finds the use of fundamentalist religious symbols such as reference to something called "the rapture" to be constraining, and she appreciates the fact that symbols of this kind are not used in Quaker discussion. She continues to participate in a small worship-sharing group on a weekly basis. She makes her own contribution in any group meeting. Surely the thought, planning, and many hours of time that Melanie has given in service to our meeting is "love made visible."

—Judy Edgerton, September 1991

QUAKER PROFILE No. 18:

Patrick Reid

Spirit, spiritual, spirituality; all of these words come from the Latin word *spiritus*, meaning breath, breath of God, inspiration. A few months ago Patrick Reid (Paddy) and his wife, Dorothy Watson, hosted weekly meetings of a small group of Bloomington Friends. The group shared on a very deep level their insights concerning things of the spirit. "I realize that my own spirituality is shaped by my childhood experiences, which are very vivid," Paddy says. "These are things that stay with you all your life."

Paddy describes his spirituality as a blend of contemplation and action. He does not understand social action without the kind of inner peace that comes from constant searching for God's will, from the inner struggle to achieve a balance between spirit and action coming together as spirituality.

And indeed this spirituality does go back to his childhood, where he lived by the waterfront in the slums of Dublin, Ireland, never able to see the natural beauty of the legendary Emerald Isle. He recalls how he wept at age ten when the rest of the family had their first trip out of the city, made possible by some charity, while he stayed behind to take care of his mother and newborn twins. "My inner-city community was a place of last resort, like Calcutta," he said. "Life was cheap; life was random and could be taken away."

He went on to speak of his grief and frustration when close relatives died because of a lack of care and available medical attention. He witnessed the death of a number of children from traffic accidents in the streets where they swarmed together because there was no other place to play. A searing childhood memory is of a baby falling from the arms of its mother who was leaning out of a window high above the street. He closed his eyes so as not to see the tiny broken body that had fallen almost where he was standing. The mother had called out to him before she dropped the child.

Paddy himself endured physical pain from the time he was born. In early childhood he spent a great deal of time hospitalized to correct a cleft palate. He still suffers the effects of that condition in the form of some hearing impairment. "Dealing with so much pain, suffering, and death, you have to ask questions," he said. "These things make you question God at a most intense level. Grab it; hold onto it; try to make sense out of it. Go on living and try to come to terms with it." He now has dreams that recall those scenes of tragedy and death and his own helplessness. He has been told that they are post-traumatic dreams. A theory from psychology is that such dreams come as a way of helping the human mind to deal with tragic reality. Paddy writes about his experiences in the form of stories and reads them to people. "It helps me to share them," he says. One of the stories is being published in the *Fort Lauderdale Quarterly*. It is entitled "The Death of a Child."

Paddy could be said to have grown to manhood without ever having been a child, in the sense that he did not live in a protected environment where he could gain confidence in the world as an orderly, dependable place. Such a childhood seems cruelly unnatural. Yet Paddy surely had an inner resiliency that gave him the strength not only to help his own family, but to begin helping those outside his family. He started helping the elderly poor during his teen years in Dublin. Much later he carried his concern across the Atlantic and worked with the elderly poor in Madison, Wisconsin. And now, here in Bloomington, it is not surprising that the date set for this profile interview was postponed by one day so that he could assist a helpless elderly man to get dressed for going to the doctor.

Paddy left school at age thirteen and worked as a laborer for four years. As the oldest in a family of six boys and two girls, he shouldered much of the responsibility for the family after the untimely death of his mother, Kathleen Bollard Reid, following the birth of the youngest child. His father, also named Patrick Reid (Paddy is the fourth Patrick) worked on the waterfront, employed only when ships came in to be unloaded and loaded. There had been hunger marches in Dublin and other parts of Ireland in the 1950s. Paddy remembers the winter of 1960 and 1961 as years when thousands were unemployed, when people died from hunger, and when his father and fellow workers brought stolen food home to their families. Stealing out of desperation meant surviving. Extended family members all helped each other. "It was a different world," he said. "There they had true community. They took care of each other — even to making sure that those who did not survive had a decent burial."

Through the 1960s conditions improved in the country, although there was still much poverty. As each child in Paddy's family grew old enough to earn some money, the family's financial situation improved. Soon after the death of Paddy's mother, the family was able to move out of the slum section and into a suburb.

At age sixteen, Paddy became an apprentice carpenter in a vocational school. As a part of his training, he was assigned to do volunteer carpentry repair work for elderly people in dire need. There he began his social action, for he did much more than the job required. He also taught people to do their own repair work. The school provided only about twenty percent of the needed materials. Paddy himself furnished materials, and some businesses helped. He continued the same kind of social action for fifteen years, up to 1980. He was also employed during four of those years by the National Transport Company, doing maintenance work in the bus station and other public facilities.

In 1972, at twenty-two years of age, Paddy entered the Catholic seminary of the Redemptorist Fathers in Galway, the best-known religious order in Ireland. With social work in the inner city so much a part of his own life, he hoped the church would become socially involved there too. He said that the seminary was not accustomed to taking students like him from the working class, and that it continued this practice for only a couple of years. The Catholic church in Ireland is conservative and opulent, he said. His experience had been that of going to soup kitchens, and at the seminary they had no knowledge of that kind of life. They did not understand him. His concept of God was different. They preached a fire-and-brimstone religion. The vow of poverty taken by the priests was really a vow of security, he said. Nevertheless, he studied at the seminary for six years, taking courses, among other things, in philosophy, sociology, and theology, and becoming almost ready for the priesthood.

In the mid-1970s Paddy spent some time working in a war-torn community in Northern Ireland. He observed that the Quaker witness is important there, saying that their impartiality makes them acceptable by both sides of the conflict. He stated that of the approximately three thousand Quakers in Ireland, two-thirds live in the Irish Republic. He first became aware of Quakers in the 1960s when one of them, the owner of a chain of excellent cafés in Dublin, Victor Bewley, turned his business over to the workers. Paddy was impressed by that action, and by accounts of the anti-slavery stance taken by nineteenth-century Quakers. From what he knew of Quakers, he was attracted by the way they alternated between contemplation and action, striking a balance, in contrast to the Eastern religious traditions such as Zen, with a purely contemplative life. He mentioned Dag Hammarskjöld's book, *Markings*, and said he was struck by the similar interaction there between mysticism and service.

Paddy often goes to the Bible, especially to his favorite part, the parables of Jesus, where he has continued to find new meanings over the years. The result is a deeper appreciation of the Christian tradition. He believes we need to take what is good and nourishing from our Western tradition. He learns to do God's will from the lives of the saints, such as the moody, strange Saint John of the Cross, who was a misunderstood outcast in his own day. His favorite saints were all nature-centered, and yet in touch with the world. He is moved by Gregorian chant. He appreciates the ancient Celtic tradition and the Irish folklore expressed in Ireland's rich heritage of poetry, prose literature, drama, and music.

Paddy quotes John Anderson, someone he knew in Madison who is now at the Pendle Hill Quaker study center in

Pennsylvania, as saying that the only true answer about belief in God is "I don't know." For Paddy a lot of life consists in saying "I don't know" and then going on. When he was little, religion was important to him, and a solace. He questioned it, but religion played an important role during those years of hardship. He was taught that there would be reward after the vale of tears — a kind of fatalism. For many years Paddy did not pray, but prayer has now become a major part of his life. It is like food and water to him. He pleads for mercy, and prays for family members, holding an image of each one in his mind.

Paddy says that in monastic life everything is centered on prayer. Since coming to Bloomington in 1990, he and Dorothy have spent some time at a small retreat house near the Gethsemane Monastery at Bardstown, Kentucky, where Thomas Merton (Father M. Louis) lived, worked with his hands, and wrote. Paddy likes the hidden ground of spirituality expressed in Thomas Merton's book, *The Hidden Ground of Love*. Paddy and Dorothy enjoy the peace and quiet of the retreat house under the care of the nun Sister Danielle.

The activism that began so early in life continued after Paddy and Dorothy arrived in Madison, Wisconsin, in 1983. Just before coming, he had been counseling and teaching carpentry skills to young offenders on parole in Dublin, under the auspices of the Catholic church. Arriving in Madison, he found a need to work helping low-income elderly people. Then a new challenge took him to Lexington, Mississippi, and during six summers he worked for civil rights among blacks in the Mississippi Delta region. Three nuns from a convent near Chicago were living and working the year round in Holmes County, Mississippi, which Paddy learned was the poorest county in the country. There Paddy helped to construct family homes. He also pulled weeds in the cotton fields in extreme heat. The setting was different, but he found the attitudes were the same as those in his home community back in Dublin.

Paddy's first actual association with Quakers was in Madison. After reading an article about the Friends Meeting in the local newspaper, he went to visit a meeting and found it to be a place of tranquillity. He was able to derive much benefit from the chance to contemplate: to sit quietly, meditate, and pray. He found the experience to be nourishing. When he encouraged discussion on grief and loss, the meeting was very supportive. Every Sunday a group met for two hours. He became a member of the Society of Friends while living in Madison.

We referred at the beginning of this profile to the meetings held in Paddy's and Dorothy's apartment here in Bloomington. Dorothy is now in her second year of teaching in the sociology department at Indiana University. The couple met in 1979 when they were at Cork University in the southern part of Ireland. Paddy was doing a survey on housing, his field of specialty, for the Combat Poverty Program funded by the European Economic Community. Dorothy was a doctoral candidate in sociology. They were married in a Catholic ceremony in Dublin in 1981. For their honeymoon, they rode bicycles over the beautiful green countryside in the midlands of Ireland.

Paddy has joined Elizabeth Buck and Haines Turner in visits to prisoners in the Monroe County Jail each Tuesday evening here in Bloomington. He appreciates this opportunity for personal contact with people in these unfortunate circumstances. At this writing he is helping with plans for a Friends Meeting retreat to be held before this profile is printed. The retreat subject concerns Quaker methods of resolving conflicts, led by Friends from New York Yearly Meeting who are experienced in leading workshops on conflict resolution with prison inmates in that state. Just last month, Paddy and Dorothy gave up their apartment and moved into a trailer park in order to be closer to people in the lower income category. Both are already involved in social service in their new neighborhood.

Exactly a year ago in October, Paddy began work leading to a master's degree in bereavement studies from Vermont College in Montpelier, Vermont. In an intensive program called Seniority Plus, under the direction of Philip Stafford at the Bloomington Hospital, Paddy is researching how Western culture views death. This includes bereavement counseling, spirituality and death, how we come to have a taboo culture on the subject of death, and why people approaching death are shunted away into nursing homes. Thus the little boy who was forced to ask the meaning of life and death in the slums of Dublin has become the mature, questing man, bringing insight with perhaps no other parallel into ultimate decisions that affect us all.

— Judy Edgerton, October 1991

QUAKER PROFILE No. 19:

Hazel Cronk Smith

She has a ready smile that easily turns into a soft chuckle, a twinkle in her dark eyes, and a pair of dimples. But do not be deceived: she is energetic, capable, and — yes, she can speak her mind. That is our Hazel Smith, who analyzes varied opinions voiced in any meeting, large or small, and brings the discussion into focus with incisive logic.

Even though Hazel might not want us to say it, she is a living example of the commandment from both the Old and the New Testaments, "Love thy neighbor as thyself." For more than forty years here in Bloomington, with her keen mind and her capable hands, she has demonstrated the meaning of that injunction.

Hazel is a birthright Friend, who grew up in the small town of Plainfield, Indiana, an hour's drive north of Bloomington and the home of Western Yearly Meeting. Her Plainfield meeting was a pastoral type, well and regularly attended each Sunday by its members. The graded, printed Sunday school lessons, with Bible texts and commentary, were studied as seriously by Hazel as was her school homework. In meeting for worship at Plainfield, a period of silence regularly followed a sermon of only twenty minutes. (Norval Webb, the pastor, said he thought everything worth saying could always be said in twenty minutes.) During the silent worship a second speech was invariably given, always by the same man and always unintelligibly. Following that, others permitted themselves to speak.

Hazel has loving memories of her parents, Howard George and Netta Moon Cronk. She feels very close to her younger sister, Barbara Cronk Diehl, who lives in Oxford, Ohio. The two sisters also feel warmly toward their younger brother, Harold Thomas, now living in California, who strictly speaking was a first cousin, but who was brought up by their parents. Barbara was only four years old when Hazel left for college, and so the sisters saw very little of each other at home. Their mother died at a relatively young age in 1949, and their father died ten years ago. In recent times, she and Barbara have grown to be very near and have kept in close communication with each other. Hazel pays tribute to Barbara's great courage through the lingering illness and death of her husband, saying that going through her sister's experience with her has been a great inspiration. Barbara has visited our meeting with Hazel several times.

Hazel describes her mother as having always been compassionate and nonjudgmental; she quotes her as saying, "Always put yourself in the other person's place." Her father loved the woods and fields, hunting game for the family table, and fishing in the streams and ponds. He took the family camping, and Hazel acquired a love of nature from him. (Husband Raymond Smith says Hazel learned to fish so well that once when they took a boat and went fishing together, Hazel let her line dangle while she read a book — and caught the only fish of the day.)

Although unquestioning during childhood, Hazel broadened her religious experience in her teen years. During that time an ecumenical experience began for her that has grown through the years and influences her outlook to this day. She believes that "no one group has the whole truth — not even the Quakers!" As a very young child in church, she said she did what she was told and believed what she was told. That changed when young people from four different denominations, each with only a few teens in their membership, formed their own organization. They gave it a name, the Christian Youth Quest Group. There were about twenty-five members from the Methodists, Disciples of Christ, Baptists, and Hazel's Society of Friends. They met in each other's homes and sometimes in one of the churches. The door was always open at the home of the Reverend and Mrs. Gilbert Daniel, of the Disciples of Christ, who had three children in that age range. Hazel remembers the Daniels' home as a place where they could have fun, and the parents as people who had a positive influence on her. The death from leukemia of Muriel Daniel, a girl near her own age, was a deep personal tragedy for Hazel.

These early ecumenical experiences prepared Hazel for working with Christians of other sects more than a decade later. During that decade she lived in three different states, without access to Quaker meetings, and that reinforced her feeling of being at home with other Christians. She became involved in volunteer social service in Bloomington at about the time our Friends Meeting was established. She was impressed by the vision and energy of a group of concerned women from a large number of local churches as they combined their efforts to help people in need. Hazel became a representative for Friends in the Council of Church Women (now Church Women United), the organization that owned the Christian Center at that time. A by-product for her has been her close personal friendships with talented people whom she admires for using their leisure and their abilities in time-consuming, sometimes difficult community service rather than for trivial self-centered pleasures.

Hazel became the secretary, then the vice-chairman, and finally served two terms as the chairman of the Christian Center Board, during which the board organized Opportunity House. She and three other people did what she terms brainstorming in preparation for the project. The idea originated with the director of the Christian Center at that time, the Reverend Paul Crafton.

The Christian Center, now known as Monroe County United Ministries (MCUM), has become well-established; its services in the community are taken for granted. Opportunity House is owned by Church Women United, and is staffed by volunteers with the exception of two persons paid to do heavy lifting. It is an outlet for used clothing, antique jewelry and glassware, and other items. All proceeds are given to Monroe County United Ministries for its varied programs benefiting needy families and individuals. For the very young there is a preschool day-care center, and at the opposite end of the life cycle a variety of meaningful activities attract the elderly. Although MCUM is staffed by a director, a social worker, teachers for the preschool, and office help, volunteers are constantly needed for a variety of tasks.

At this writing, Hazel is in her second year of a three-year term representing Opportunity House on the board of MCUM. She is scheduled to work at the House two full eight-hour days each week, and is co-chairman of a committee that researches the value of antique items donated for sale.

Working closely with Paul Crafton and his wife Susie in implementing the plans for starting Opportunity House and also in expanding the services at the Christian Center, Hazel came to have a rare appreciation for their lives of dedication, and says they literally burned themselves out. She also recalls with appreciation the help and inspiration of the late Reverend Douglas Rae of the First Baptist Church.

Although knowing these women and men has reinforced the ecumenical influences of her early years, Hazel is steeped in Quakerism by upbringing and by reason of being a graduate of Earlham College at Richmond, Indiana. She was there in the mid-1930s at a time when much of the country was struggling with racial discrimination. An incident over a weekend trip home gave Hazel the opportunity to demonstrate her own lack of prejudice. At Earlham she was one of three young women in a large dormitory room. When one of the three dropped out of school, Hazel and the other roommate invited a girl of mixed parentage — half Native American and half African-American — to join them. The three got along well, and Hazel invited both roommates home with her and took them to Indianapolis to see a motion picture. When she bought the three tickets, the ticket seller said, gesturing to the dark-skinned friend, "What about that girl?" Hazel replied that one of the tickets was for her.

"She can't come in here."

"All right, then — we'll go to the theater down the street."

But her friend, who was from Massachusetts, said, "I won't be allowed in there either."

So they returned home to the movie theater in Plainfield, where blacks were allowed only upstairs in the balcony but where Hazel and her two friends were seated downstairs because, she said, people knew her.

Earlham students were making a concerted effort at that time to encourage integration, Hazel said. For instance, the basketball team walked out of a restaurant where the one black member of the Earlham team was refused seating.

At Earlham, Hazel took a course in Quaker history along with her major in English and Speech. "I'm not a religious philosopher," she says. "I simply live each day as best I can." She refers appreciatively to Errol Elliott's book, *Quakers on the American Frontier*. She likes the humorously written philosophy of Tom Mullen's books, *Where Two or Three are Gathered Together, Someone Spills the Milk,* and *Laughing Out Loud and Other Religious Experiences*. She also likes Wilmer Cooper's recent study of Quakerism, *A Living Faith*.

Hazel was one of the six Quakers who got together in 1950 and organized the Bloomington Friends Meeting, under the care of Blue River Monthly Meeting. When our meeting decided to look for a permanent home (after gathering first in the homes of individual members, then in the tower of the Indiana Memorial Union, then in space belonging to the Indiana School of Religion at the University, and finally at the Seventh Day Adventist Church), it was Hazel — along with her husband, Raymond Smith —who found the little dwelling house situated on some partly wooded, rolling acreage on Moores Pike, that became the Bloomington Friends meetinghouse in 1968.

Hazel has been clerk of Ministry and Counsel, recording clerk of the meeting, and also recording clerk of Blue River Quarterly Meeting. At the present time she is serving on two important Meeting committees: Nominating, and Property and Finance.

Hazel speaks appreciatively of the leadership provided at this time by Robert Schutt as clerk of the meeting and Peter Burkholder as recording clerk. She likes having someone actively in charge of all events, rather than trusting that things will go well without guidance. She misses the warmth and closeness of the early days when the meeting was smaller. She likes to have meetings for worship be meetings for worship, with everyone leaving worldly things that divide us at the meetinghouse door.

Hazel speaks of the bombing of Pearl Harbor on December 7, 1941, and of our nation's entry into the Second World War as a turning point in her life. Like most Americans, she had been brought up to believe that World War I was fought to end all wars, and she was shocked and bewildered. She says that Pearl Harbor and Hitler's genocide raised a serious question for her. "The Quaker peace testimony is an ideal to strive for, but I wonder about its absolute applicability. When people are absolutely defenseless, as the Jews were in Germany and Poland; when they come up against those who have no conscience. . ." Her sentence remains unfinished, an expression of the dilemma faced by many people who continue to work toward the ideal.

Hazel and Raymond were married in September 1938 after having graduated in the same class at Earlham in June. They spent their first year of marriage in Bloomington, where she did substitute teaching while Raymond earned a master's degree. Beginning in the fall of 1940, she fully enjoyed a privileged social life in a college community in Valley City, North Dakota, where Raymond taught at North Dakota State Teachers College. Then came that fateful day in December 1941 and, she says, "things were never the same again." They moved to Madison, Wisconsin, where Raymond taught in the Army Air Force Radio School, later transferring to Belleville, Illinois. Then he was drafted into the army and assigned to teach at Scott Field in Illinois. All the while Hazel taught first kindergarten, and then all eight grades, in a one-room school. In 1946, Raymond was invited to return to Indiana University as an instructor in speech. Hazel and Raymond have lived in Bloomington ever since, except for a year's leave of absence for Raymond to complete his doctorate at the University of Wisconsin.

Since his retirement from the university as Professor of Speech, Raymond has preferred a quiet life pursuing his varied and complicated hobbies: hybridization of irises, experimental breeding of rabbits, and making violins. Hazel enjoys life in their tastefully decorated modern home in a suburban setting when her busy outside schedule allows her to be there, but her volunteer social work continues unabated. Her natural calm has sometimes been sorely tested, such as when vandals broke the large front windows at Opportunity House, or when they set fire to a Dumpster, resulting in the destruction of one of the buildings used for storage and sorting, which then had to be replaced at considerable cost.

We at the Meeting appreciate her valuable outreach done in the name of Bloomington Friends. Paraphrasing George Fox's statement early in his ministry, any woman or man who sets forth in the spirit of the prophets and apostles can shake all the country for ten miles around.

— Judy Edgerton, November 1991

QUAKER PROFILE No. 20:

Sandra Key Wolf Nichols

> Being Friends is a part of our lives, Jim and I — we wouldn't *not* do it.
>
> — Sandy Nichols

For one who has lived not much over half the biblical "threescore years and ten," Sandy has had a remarkable religious and practical journey. It seems to have been inevitable that she would be in the forefront of the now widely acclaimed truth that the proper nurture of children is the solution to society's ills. The foundation for that has been with Sandy from her own formative years growing up in Oklahoma.

Right now Sandy is in the midst of day-to-day parenting — using her intelligence and insight, and drawing on her unusual experiences in childhood and the unique responsibilities she had in her work as a young adult — all of it combined with a sensitivity to human needs. She and her husband, James Tyler Nichols, who is a doctoral candidate in Library Science at Indiana University, are the parents of twelve-year-old James Key Nichols and seven-year-old Andrew Tyler Nichols.

After asking Sandy to be the subject for a profile, we read an article in the November 1991 issue of *Quaker Life* entitled "The Peaceful Way of Raising Children." The author gives credit to conversations with Sandy "on raising a peaceful child." Sandy was surprised when we showed her the article, and then obligingly went through it and identified passages that she recalls having expressed as her philosophy.

Sandy describes her own trial-and-error experience when son James was little more than a toddler. She and Jim took him with them when they participated in demonstrations for causes about which they had strong convictions. They stopped taking him when they discovered that the little boy was being asked about his parents' views at these demonstrations, even by representatives of the news media. "He was being exploited," she said. "As he grew older, he was having to answer for my actions, and it wasn't fair."

Sensitivity to the needs of her children is reflected in this description of herself: "I am the strictest parent I know, but in a different way. I don't scream or spank. I expect them to understand and to act on it. Some Friends ask why we impose our will on the children if we don't on other adults. My answer is that we are teaching our children concern, politeness, a general caring for others. Something is wrong if children are so wild that there is no peace in the home and others are disturbed." She went on to talk about the importance of being a peaceful parent, about monitoring outside influences such as television, and about sharing the love of God with the child. In their home Sandy, Jim, and their children have a period of worshipful silence before each meal; they hold a longer period of quiet together when someone is facing a crisis: for example, when their son James was grieving over the death of a pet rabbit.

Then Sandy talked about her own childhood — her parents, Key Wolf, Jr., and Nina Marie (Nodine) Wolf; her two younger sisters, Karen and Keyla; and the "strange collection of people," ranging from newborn infants to teenagers, who spent some time as a part of their family. Her father worked for the Bureau of Indian Affairs as director of Child Welfare Services for several counties in Oklahoma. "It was difficult to place children in foster homes, and we kept those that no one else would take — some of them for as long as a year," Sandy said. "Some of the young teens were pregnant; one baby was born in our home. All the children were unfortunate. My mother never said no to any young person who needed to stay with us. She still keeps in touch with children who lived with us till adoption."

Sandy's father, Key Wolf, Jr., was the son of Grover Cleveland Howlingwolf, a Chickasaw Indian who was also known as Key Wolf, Sr. ("Key" comes from the Chickasaw word for "howling.") This man, her grandfather, was an orphan, a victim of the forced Indian resettlement from the southeastern United States into Oklahoma that is referred to in history books as the Trail of Tears. They were given a large part of the Oklahoma Territory in common. Then in her grandfather's preteen years the government took the lands and enrolled the Indians as tribal members, allotting each of them one hundred acres. Sandy's grandfather was given his name at the time of his enrollment. Sandy's mother has Cherokee ancestry. They too were part of the forced resettlement from rich, fertile lands between the Appalachians and the Mississippi into arid Oklahoma.

In 1907 Sandy's grandfather became the first Indian to graduate from the University of Oklahoma. He had sold a part of his hundred-acre allotment of land to finance his education. Sandy's grandmother was white, a member of a Methodist church. Key Wolf, Sr., felt that speaking the Chickasaw language would be an obstacle for his seven children in becoming a part of the mainstream culture. He put a high value on education, and all seven children graduated from college. Sandy's father, one of the seven, was a graduate of the University of Oklahoma in social work and psychology, and earned a Ph.D. degree when she was in early grade school.

Sandy says she grew up in a dual culture, but remarked that it is hard to keep an Indian identity in a predominantly white society. In Oklahoma the family lived at various times in Norman, Ardmore, and Pawhuska. They also lived for one year each on two different reservations — the Shoshone-Blackfoot in Idaho, and another reservation in North Dakota. On one of those reservations Sandy and her sister had trouble being accepted at school because Sandy's eyes are blue and Karen's are hazel, but there was no doubt that they really belonged after their dark-skinned, black-haired father went over to the school to prove it. Still, Sandy adds, she really grew up in a predominantly white culture.

Sandy's father was deeply religious and took his children to different Protestant churches, but never found what he was looking for. The support of his wife in taking care of the three children and the many homeless ones over the years enabled him to carry on his social work in spite of a heart ailment that had appeared in his youth. He died almost fourteen years ago.

Sandy's youngest sister, Keyla, a Cherokee Indian, is adopted. She was found as an abandoned baby, about five weeks old, in a motel room in a dresser drawer, near death from malnutrition and dehydration. Evidently she had been there for as long as three or four days. As a result, she has had both psychological and physical problems over the years. She is now very ill in a nursing facility. Although Keyla gets disability income from Social Security, Sandy's mother (now remarried) has the full responsibility for her. Keyla's biological parents have found the whereabouts of their daughter. The birth mother has been more disruptive than helpful, and the father has not been able to take any responsibility. All this continues to be a great heartache for Sandy and those in her family.

Sandy describes her parents as being good role models. Her father was "very liberal — embarrassingly so," she says. They were an unconventional family, living by their own principles regardless of the dictates of society. In adulthood, she discovered that she could easily identify with the Society of Friends. "I found nothing unusual in Quakerism," she explained.

Sandy has an undergraduate degree in education from the University of Oklahoma, and was a candidate for the master's degree in library science there in 1973 when she met Jim during his work as a doctoral candidate in English. She started going to the unprogrammed Oklahoma City Friends Meeting, which Jim was already attending. "We knew it was the place for us," she said. Jim had his first contact with Friends when he became a conscientious objector in his teen years, during the Vietnam War, and was counseled by various religious leaders, including Quakers, in Bartlesville, Oklahoma.

Jim and Sandy were married in 1975 under the care of Oklahoma City Friends Meeting. Sandy had moved to Denver, Colorado, where she was data coordinator for the American Indian Commission on Alcohol and Drug Abuse, funded by the Indian Health Service. Jim joined her in Denver and enrolled at the University of Denver in mass communications studies. The staff of the commission where Sandy was employed was made up exclusively of people of Indian ancestry and was the parent organization for 162 local groups — small drug and alcohol clinics all over the country. As data coordinator, Sandy used her library training to set up an information-retrieval system. She organized all the files and the finances, and edited the newsletter. After two and a half years, she went on to a job at the National Indian Health Board, made up of twelve people, each representing a geographic region that contained one or more tribes. The job of the NIHB was to monitor health issues for the American Indian, to bring the needs to the attention of the Indian Health Service at the national level, and to organize national conferences. Sandy was charged with writing a position paper for American Indians on national health insurance. This responsibility required her to travel across the country to meet with representatives of all the tribes. She explained plans for a program of national health insurance to them. Their health care varied in quality but in general was poor. However, they were receiving it at no cost and were therefore reluctant to move to a system of health insurance.

Sandy gave up this work in 1979 when she and Jim moved to La Junta, Colorado, where he did a media program as part of the curriculum for a nursing school at Otero Junior College. Their first child, James, was born while they were there. Following that, Boulder was home for a year while Jim worked at the University of Colorado library. He then enrolled at the University of Denver for a master's degree in library science. In 1981, he became service librarian for Indiana University East, and they moved to Richmond, Indiana. There they were members of Clear Creek Friends Meeting. In

1984, the year their son Andrew was born, Jim became director of the library at Wilmington College in Ohio.

This past August (1991), the family moved from Wilmington to Bloomington for Jim's doctoral program at the university. Our Friends meeting has welcomed Jim and Sandy and their sons as sojourners from Campus Friends Meeting at Wilmington College, which is a united meeting, affiliated with both Ohio Valley Yearly Meeting in the Friends General Conference and Wilmington Yearly Meeting in Friends United Meeting. Both Sandy and Jim have been active in Ohio Valley Yearly Meeting. For three years Sandy was clerk of the Advancement committee, which serves basically as Ministry and Counsel for the Yearly Meeting. The annual sessions of Ohio Valley Yearly Meeting are always residential, gathering every other year at Wilmington College and at other locations in alternate years. The Advancement committee decides on a theme for the sessions, invites a speaker, and plans workshops around the chosen theme. There is worship sharing every day, and morning and evening worship. As clerk of the Advancement committee, Sandy made all arrangements for the site, whether at Wilmington or elsewhere. She speaks of the worship and fellowship at these residential yearly meetings as an invaluable experience.

Before her three years with the Advancement committee, Sandy spent three years as clerk of the Junior Yearly Meeting committee. The Junior meetings consisted of both young children and older Young Friends. That part of the yearly meeting grew so rapidly that it was necessary to divide into two committees. "A fun part of the program," she says, "included a pizza party for the children and a dinner party for adults to celebrate birthdays." Ninety to one hundred people stay for all five days of the Yearly Meeting sessions, with a total attendance including drop-ins of 120 to 170. In addition, Ohio Valley has a women's group of ten to twenty who meet informally two or three times a year for dinner and an overnight slumber party.

Sandy found time last year to take a course at Wilmington College in comparative religion — Social Change and Nonviolence: Woolman and Gandhi, taught by Sterling Olmstead. She is inspired by the writings of Thomas Kelly. While attending worship-sharing groups in Richmond she formed a spiritual friendship with Howard Alexander, a professor of mathematics at Earlham who late in his career also earned an M.A. in religion at the Earlham School of Religion. She regularly reads Pendle Hill pamphlets. One that has been especially meaningful is *On Hallowing One's Diminishments,* written by John Youngblut and published in 1990. She has found his message helpful in dealing with grief for her terminally ill sister, and with an ongoing tragedy for which there seems to be no solution involving a member of Jim's family.

Sandy is pleased by the way James, in sixth grade, and Andrew, in first, are being challenged at University School here in Bloomington. Although Jim's schedule at the university keeps him so busy that she is "like a single parent," she says he loves his work. After moving from a sizable house in Wilmington, so far, her own challenge has largely been trying to make a small apartment in university housing into a comfortable home for her family. We sense that Sandy may not yet have found her own niche in her new framework, but her hearty, infectious laugh leaves no doubt that she will. She has joined our Religious Education committee, and we are glad to see the family in attendance together at meetings for worship. We claim them joyfully as our own while they are with us, and hope they will stay for a very long time.

—Judy Edgerton, December 1991

QUAKER PROFILE No. 21:

JoAnna Nix Henegar

There are no words to describe the great room with its ceiling that seems to soar endlessly, and with its high walls broken by a surrounding balcony that forms a reassuring embrace. This is what one sees upon entering Riley Children's Hospital, which is part of the Indiana University Medical Center in Indianapolis. Children who are ill and parents who suffer with them surely gain courage from the light pouring in through the overhead skylight, the cheerful colors used on the painted walls, and the larger-than-life animal figures from children's literature perched on the corners of the balcony railings.

We had the reassuring experience of sitting in this room one rainy afternoon after making an out-patient visit to another part of the hospital complex. Not quite three years later we learned in conversation with JoAnna Nix Henegar that she was the designer responsible for planning artwork throughout the hospital. It was part of a major new addition to Riley Children's Hospital, dedicated in 1987.

JoAnna said that her work as interior designer for Indiana University has been a major influence in her life. The responsibility of her department in designing for over twenty million square feet of space in the university's buildings all over the state of Indiana created a work load for her and her staff that she describes as overwhelming. "But," she added, "it is really rewarding to design things and then get to see the results." There are major examples of her work on the Bloomington campus, especially in the Memorial Union Building, and in all the campus libraries — including the main library. The interior of the law library is JoAnna's creation, including the functional furnishings that she designed.

We asked JoAnna whether she thought being a Friend influenced her working life in any way. We would expect Quaker traits like simplicity and honesty in function to be evident in such artistic expression. This turned out to be so, for she said that she had sometimes been at odds with people wanting design to be ostentatious or to serve as a symbol of status. "I want things simple, pleasing, and durable," she said.

As with many thinking people in the 1950s, JoAnna and her husband Warren Henegar were faced with uneasiness when the extreme right-wing anticommunist movement grew strong during the McCarthy period. As JoAnna said, "Things did not make sense." They were living then in Eugene, Oregon, after their marriage in 1951 in San Francisco. They were attracted to the Society of Friends by the approach of the American Friends Service Committee to problems in the world, "an approach to problems," as JoAnna said, "other than spouting cold-war lines." They heard an AFSC representative speak in a radio interview about the direction taken by Quakers in dealing with the Soviet Union and Eastern Europe. She and Warren decided to look up Quakers there in Eugene. They contacted the clerk of the unprogrammed meeting and then took their young baby Lillian with them to their first Friends meeting. It was held in a large house belonging to the Wesley Foundation. "There were great people in that meeting," she said. "I still think the greatest thing about the Society of Friends is the Friends." She and Warren stayed in Eugene for two and a half years, during which time she was working for a photogrammetrist as a draftsman and Warren was employed by the U.S. Social Security Administration.

In 1955 Warren was transferred to Bakersfield, California, where they were visited by a representative of the Welcome Wagon, who proudly recited the names of all the churches in the vicinity. The woman was puzzled when JoAnna asked about a Quaker meeting, but being eager to please, she offered: "We do have an Aimee Semple McPherson Church of the Foursquare Gospel!"

Late in the 1950s, Warren and JoAnna exchanged the West Coast for the East Coast and moved to Baltimore, Maryland, the headquarters for Social Security. All during those years in Oregon and California, they had felt drawn to the care and cultivation of a piece of the good earth: to farming. While they lived in Maryland, JoAnna's mother, Clara Irene Huggins Nix, played an important role in the young couple's future. She ordered a farm real-estate catalog for them that listed farms for sale all over the United States. Basic intellectuals that they were, JoAnna and Warren asked questions and did research in preparation for making a choice. They were impressed by an article in *Harper's* magazine that recommended a small town with a large university, not close to a military base or to major industry or to a large highway. JoAnna and Warren thought they would also find Quakers in a university town. There was the excitement of adventure in JoAnna's voice as she described the decision to choose a place from the whole country where they would put down their roots — both literally and figuratively. Next came on-site exploration. Two more children, Anna and Alice, had been added to the family by the time they were ready to start visiting potential sites. Louisville, Kentucky, was on the list. That city had the misfortune of offering only a drizzling rain while they desperately searched for, and eventually found, an elusive laundry for their babies' diapers. As they drove across the Ohio River to New Albany, the sun came out on them and their freshly diapered babies — an omen of welcome to the state of Indiana.

Wanting a closer look at the state, they decided to take a vacation in Bloomington, a place recommended by a good friend back in Oregon who had relatives living there. The exact date when they first saw Bloomington and the surrounding countryside — May 4, 1957 — remains fixed in JoAnna's memory. "It was beautiful, with redbud and dogwood in bloom," she said. Immediately after that vacation, Warren asked to be transferred to Bloomington. The transfer came through in only three weeks.

The farm they found is located just south of Bloomington. In late October they closed the deal. In January 1958, with the thermometer standing at three degrees below zero, they moved into the existing house — which had cracks in the walls wide enough for the light to come through. Showing the same innovative talents she later employed in overcoming difficult problems as interior designer at the university, JoAnna arranged for her family's comfort by shutting off all but two rooms heated by a coal stove. They used water from a pump that often froze, and they learned to recycle water used for rinsing dishes by reheating it after the next meal and washing the dishes in it. What is more, she said, the children had not a single cold all that winter!

Of course they found Bloomington Friends Meeting, then only eight years old and still gathering for worship in rented space. She and Warren immediately became active in the meeting. She says of herself, "I'm compulsive. I get involved." A good illustration took place in 1960, when she was seven months pregnant with her daughter Jane. Advanced pregnancy did not keep her from joining other Friends and sympathizers from all over the country in Washington, D.C., where they formed a human chain encircling the Pentagon in protest against looming threats of a Vietnam war. The event coincided with the commemoration of the 300th anniversary of the Peace Testimony of the Society of Friends.

Longtime Friends in Bloomington remember with pleasure the meetings for worship at the Henegar farm three or four times a year, which began with breakfast and then were held outside under a large shade tree. In the intervening years since then, they have hosted Easter egg hunts, potluck picnics, and nature hikes for Meeting members and attenders.

JoAnna was born in Dallas, Texas. She says that generations of her ancestors had lived on the frontier. Her ability to create order and beauty in art and everyday life and her positive attitude toward the people she meets have their origins in her family; she was the youngest of three children in the oil-rich panhandle region of northeastern Texas. JoAnna's father, George Estley Nix, was an oil-driller who not only worked at established sites but at times did exploratory drilling for new wells (known as "wildcatting"). Before JoAnna was born, when her brother George Jordan Nix and sister Lillian Nix Cook were young children, the family lived in boomtowns where new oil wells were being put into operation. Her parents became skilled at creating comfortable homes out of new shell houses, sometimes living in tents at first. JoAnna spent her growing-up years in Pampa, Texas, while in grade school, then lived for one year in Oplin, and graduated from Borger High School. She said her parents treated hardships as adventures, and they enjoyed whatever came. They so valued friendships, never saying anything negative about other people, that JoAnna was grown before she realized any of her relatives had faults!

As a child JoAnna was "very involved and devout," she said, never questioning the religious teachings of her Baptist church. But in her early teens she began asking about things that puzzled her. She found that church people wanted her to take things on faith, putting her off and leaving her unsatisfied. It was years later, when she discovered Quakerism, that she was able to describe her dilemma as her church's "failure to speak to my condition."

JoAnna looks back on a happy childhood, and she remembers great teachers in her school experience. After high school graduation, she left the open countryside for the study of architecture at Texas Technological University in Lubbock. Her early work experience was in San Francisco. From there she went to work at Yosemite National Park, where she eventually became decorator in an elegant old hotel, the Ahwanee. Her father died in 1948, and she returned to Texas and lived with her mother. In 1951 she went back to San Francisco, joining friends whom she had known at Texas Tech. There she found her life changed one evening when she and her friends went to a Civil Rights Congress rally in a black Baptist church to support a black man who had been sentenced to be executed in Mississippi. At this meeting her friends introduced her to two brothers. One of them was Warren Henegar. They were married three months later.

From her first contact with Friends back in Oregon, JoAnna has appreciated the "freedom of each person to search for their own truth. Because of Friends' approach, we agree on essential things while allowing for diversity in nonessentials. Friends meeting is much more satisfying to me than forms of worship that we think of as traditional." Besides personal contact with Friends, JoAnna has been impressed by the writings of John Woolman, George Fox, William James, and Martin Buber. She is acquainted with the Bible, her favorite quotation being from the book of Micah: "What doth the Lord require of thee, but to do justly, and to love mercy, and to walk humbly with thy God?"

JoAnna took early retirement from Indiana University in 1988 and spent the next four months in Santa Barbara, California, where she and her sister personally cared for their beloved mother until she moved into a nursing-care facility shortly before her death.

Since JoAnna's retirement the emphases have changed, but the pace of her life has not slowed as much as she might have expected after the twenty-five years of her demanding career at the university. She and Warren have recently added two new rooms to their home. Outside landscaping includes new flower beds and a new barn. In addition to five Thoroughbred horses, they have acquired a donkey to serve as a mount for riding lessons for their six grandchildren. Beef cattle have always grazed in their green, rock-strewn meadows. They have never been without a good vegetable garden in summer, growing such a variety that some names would be unfamiliar to most people. Warren knows how to find mushrooms in the woods in early spring, and JoAnna knows how to recognize and prepare a variety of wild greens.

JoAnna was a member of our meeting's Peace and Social Concerns committee for several years in the 1960s, when the leadership of the country was setting the stage for the Vietnam War. The committee held discussions that included people from outside the meeting, and then became a community-wide peace forum that lasted throughout the war. Her leadership continued in the 1970s when she was made clerk of the meeting. She now shares her expertise as a member of the meeting's Long Range Planning committee, and serves on the Property and Finance committee. She speaks of membership in the Society of Friends as being one of great freedom to search wherever one is led, but at the same time one of great responsibility. Her participation in the life of the meeting for more than thirty years illustrates that statement.

— Judy Edgerton, January 1992

QUAKER PROFILE No. 22:

Dorothy Lynn Autenrieth Day

Quaker profiles of two members of the Day family, Ruth and Rachel, have already appeared in these pages. There are four more with the same name who are associated with Friends in Bloomington: Ruth and Rachel's parents and grandparents. This profile is of Dorothy Lynn Autenrieth Day, mother of Ruth and Rachel, wife of Mark Tyler Day, and daughter-in-law of Ted and Bettyclaire Day.

Dorothy (Dottie) describes herself as a juggler. She keeps a variety of balls in the air with remarkable success, giving Mark credit as co-juggler from the beginning of their marriage in 1964, between Dottie's third and fourth years at the University of Chicago. They have had diverse experiences together, first while they both earned undergraduate and master's degrees from the University of Chicago; later, during two years of living in an enigmatic foreign culture in Saudi Arabia, taking their two young daughters with them; then during the hardships of family separation on two occasions when Dottie went alone to do research first in Taiwan and then in mainland China; and finally in the universal human experience of bringing up their children and in their seeking together for religious insight by participation in the Society of Friends.

The juggling pattern has taken varied forms over the years. Right now Dottie is both a student in a post-master's specialist program in the School of Library and Information Sciences at Indiana University, and a half-time University Computing Services employee as a lead consultant for Public

Facilities Computing. Her work consists of the supervision of two computer sites, keeping track of computer maintenance, training consultants, and answering questions. Self-taught, she has become skilled in computer technology and is part of an international network of specialists in the field. In her course work she is concentrating on improving her skills and is taking some programming.

Dottie and Mark's course work at the University of Chicago paralleled each other, and they were also brought together by a mutual interest in music. They met in an informal singing group, loosely made up of people from the United Christian Fellowship and others at the university, when Dottie was a first-year student and Mark a second-year student.

Dottie's undergraduate program in political science required the study of a non-Western civilization. She chose China. Through Mark's choice of Islamic culture to fulfill this requirement, he became interested in the religious philosophy of his professor of Islamic civilization, who was a member of the Society of Friends. The professor believed that by understanding another faith you gain a deeper appreciation for your own. Dottie and Mark explored Quakerism together at 57th Street Meeting in Chicago, and found it to be a welcome contrast to listening to a minister who has been paid to talk. They liked the atmosphere of simply listening, and of acceptance without argumentation. Dottie appreciated the opportunity to get to know people in the meeting, especially in small worship-sharing groups, and feels that getting acquainted with other Friends is an important element in a meaningful meeting for worship.

Upon the completion of work for their M.A. degrees in library science, both she and Mark were recruited in 1968 for the Library of Congress intern program, but they turned down an offer when the nepotism rule meant that only Mark would have the opportunity. Subsequently, they were both hired as librarians at the University of New Brunswick in Canada. Next they worked as librarians at Princeton University in New Jersey. A by-product of their two years at Princeton was the opportunity for Dottie to audit classes in Chinese. They liked the experience of meeting for worship held in a historic old meetinghouse dating back to the 1700s. The meeting's location outside the town of Princeton, however, meant that a special effort was required to provide opportunities to get to know other members and attenders.

Their first child, Ruth, was born at the end of their stay in Princeton. During that time, they felt drawn to the idea of intentional communities and were led to consult with the Friends Council on Education in Philadelphia about Quaker schools. The result was an assignment to teach at The Meeting School in Rindge, New Hampshire. Dottie, Mark, and their young baby lived in a house with six high school students. In all, there were eight faculty families and about forty-five students. It turned out to be an intense experience, working in an isolated farm boarding school for adolescents and pre-adolescents, run entirely on the principle of Quaker consensus. A collection of minutes, made by students and faculty using the principle of consensus, became the rules for the school. These rules could also be changed by consensus. Each new student or faculty member was painstakingly introduced to the process. Most students persevered and learned; some faculty were dedicated and remained for some years. Farm duties were rotated, including care of cows and chickens. It added up to an exhausting regimen of down-to-earth living and learning for everyone involved. Summing up, Dottie said: "People were supportive of each other. They appreciated what people *did* rather than dwelling on what they *didn't* do."

Dottie and Mark valued the experience they gained at The Meeting School but felt it was best to get back into the field of their training, and they came to Indiana University in 1972. They were attracted by the university's doctoral program in library science, and by its offerings in Chinese for Dottie and Arabic for Mark. They were, of course, welcome additions to Bloomington Friends Meeting. The following year a second daughter, Rachel, was born.

In 1977 their routine of work and study was broken by what started as an exchange between Indiana University and Riyadh University in Saudi Arabia — a chance for Mark to immerse himself in the language and culture of the country. It is a man's university, Dottie said, and women cannot apply; in the end Mark made his own complicated arrangements to take his family with him. His work consisted in setting up government documents in the Riyadh University library, and he received a stipend for housing. They arrived in the intense heat at the end of August, lived briefly in a hotel before finding an apartment, and then discovered that Rachel, four, and Ruth, six, could not attend public school because they knew no Arabic, and the official American school was too expensive. Dottie describes their struggle to improvise a homelike atmosphere for the family in the midst of a mystifying situation in which they were no longer able to make decisions for themselves. Things seemed to have a way of turning out better than expected, but they still could not make any plans. Dottie said it was an experience in which they learned patience. During that first year, the problem of the children's schooling was solved in ingenious ways. They finally attended a private Arabic school near the library, whose Syrian and Lebanese teachers also knew English. During their second year they were able to attend a small school in the home of a woman from England, with a truly international student body.

Coincidentally, another couple from Bloomington Friends Meeting, Betty and Millard Qualls, were in Saudi Arabia that first year. Millard Qualls was teaching at Taif, some distance away. When the Qualls invited them over for Thanksgiving dinner, the Day family had the adventure of crossing an expanse of desert in order to get there. Dottie describes how they made a fireplace at Christmas using colored construction paper, and how the girls celebrated Halloween by scurrying from room to room in their own apartment. An American woman married to an Arab steered them to an "unofficially recognized" Christian church service held on Fridays, which is the Sabbath there. Mostly Europeans, some Americans from Texas, and also some Syrian and Egyptian Christians attended these services. Later, after the Iranian revolution, the group was disbanded under pressure from reactionary Saudi leaders except for small meetings in homes.

During those two years Mark developed his ability to use the spoken language, and Dottie worked on medieval Chinese short stories. A Chinese engineering company asked her to teach English, and she practiced Chinese in conversation with one of her students. At the end of her teaching program, the Chinese engineering company rewarded her with the gift of a round-trip ticket to Taiwan so that she could accept a scholarship she had won to the National Taiwan Normal University. One of her students made arrangements for her to stay with a family he knew. After returning home from Saudi Arabia in 1979 and getting her family settled, she left for Taiwan and spent nine months at Taiwan Normal University, taking courses in Chinese and teaching English on the side.

Four years later, Dottie went to China on an exchange program between Indiana University and Shandong University. She had taken her preliminary examinations for the Ph.D. in August before leaving for China in September. The university is in northern China, on the east coast at the end of the Yellow River. It is an eight-hour overnight trip from Beijing. Her research involved concentrated work on a novel, chosen as the subject for her dissertation. After some time, the university took the foreign students on a trip to the old city of Luoyang, and then down to Sichuan Province, to a beautiful section where they climbed mountains and encountered Buddhist sculpture in the hillsides on the way. That experience gave her the confidence to take some trips by herself, to buy tickets and make arrangements for places to stay on her own initiative. She said she was fortunate to be there during a year when tensions were eased and the Chinese were not afraid to have contacts with foreigners. The natural contacts with the friendly people she met on these trips improved her spoken Chinese. Over Christmas and New Year's she went to Nanjing, Hangzhou, and Shanghai. In early April she went to Dunhuang in northwest China to see caves that contained Buddhist sculptures and scriptures on scrolls dating from the Tang Dynasty in the seventh to tenth centuries. These caves had been sealed off until their discovery in this century. The frescoes were beautiful, she said, and she enjoyed her guide's stories and the undivided attention she received because the tourist season had not yet begun. She was reunited with her family at home in June of 1985.

Dottie says that she and Mark have had to make choices. They have always supported each other in their parallel careers, studying and working at the same time. They each got into their fields — Arabic and Chinese — because in general people do not understand other cultures.

The same in-depth exploration that has characterized Dottie's chosen study of Chinese language and culture has shown itself in her approach to Quakerism. She feels fortunate to have had a good childhood and early-youth foundation. She and five sisters and one brother went to a Methodist church with their parents, William George Autenrieth and Frances Oldham Autenrieth, in Omaha, Nebraska, where she was born and grew up. She was active in the Methodist Youth Fellowship. She recalls an impressionable week at the age of fifteen when she attended an MYF conference held at Purdue University in Indiana, where she was a delegate from Omaha, and afterward wrote a lengthy paper on the conference. At summer MYF camp the program included a half-hour of silence, and Dottie sometimes went off alone for more meditation. As part of the Christian Mission Witness in Nebraska, young people did a one-week door-to-door survey on religious preferences and also painted the church. Dottie says, "Kids doing these things together for religious purposes create very intense impressions."

Dottie also sang alto in the church choir. She is a good musician, as is her mother, a pianist who has kept up her music through the years. Dottie played the bass viol with the Youth Symphony Orchestra in Omaha and with the University of Chicago orchestra, and she has also played here with the Bloomington Symphony. The Autenrieths are a musical family, with several instrumentalists among the seven children. All seven are college graduates and some, including Dottie, hold advanced degrees.

Dottie's early religious experiences were broadened by the philosophical content of her liberal arts education at the University of Chicago, where the modified curriculum had been formulated earlier by Mortimer Adler, professor of the Philosophy of Law, and President Robert M. Hutchins. Through Western Civilization courses in the humanities, Dottie read books by great religious philosophers, among them Thomas Aquinas and Martin Luther. She found that her ideas about religion were brought into focus by the simple writings of the

Quaker leader Rufus M. Jones. She singled out "The Historical and Inward Christ," "Atonement," and "Prayer," included in Rufus Jones's book of essays *The Double Search.* Thomas Kelly's *Testament of Devotion* is also meaningful for her.

Ruth came home in December for the midyear holidays from Carleton College, and Rachel from Smith College. The four Days then made a trip to Texas to visit Dottie's parents, who have retired there from Omaha. They had another Christmas celebration with Ted and Bettyclaire when they returned to Bloomington. We appreciate the presence of the Day family in our family of Friends and are grateful for their participation in the life of our meeting.

— Judy Edgerton, February 1992

QUAKER PROFILE No. 23:

Phyllis Mary Wright Martin

An in-depth conversation with Phyllis Martin revealed a cosmopolitan person. She is at home on three continents: Europe, including Scotland (the place where she was born and brought up), England (where she studied), and central Europe (where she did research); Africa, where she lived, traveled, taught, and has done extensive research; and North America, where she has lived and worked in the United States since 1968, and where her sister and mother now live in Canada.

A constant from childhood down to the present has been a religious orientation and the attendant social responsibilities. Phyllis's father, the late Allan Wright, was a Baptist minister. Her mother, Mary Wright, was trained to be a teacher; but instead of teaching, she used her skills and energies in a variety of responsibilities to the church and her own family. Phyllis said that growing up in a religious household had an important influence on her. She saw in her parents truly religious people who followed the biblical precept to love one's neighbor as oneself. She remembers that her father visited people in prison, and gave money to beggars who came to the door. The family lived in Glasgow until Phyllis was seven years old, and then they moved to Edinburgh, where she went to school and where she lived until she finished her undergraduate work at Edinburgh University.

The imprint of Phyllis's childhood impressions fixed the pattern for both her religious and her professional life. She is now an associate professor in the history department at Indiana University, teaching courses in African history, women's history, and world history. She has written a number of scholarly articles and is the author, co-author, or co-editor of several books. Among these is a book entitled *Africa*, co-edited with Professor Patrick O'Meara, the director of African Studies at Indiana University. This book, which has now nearly exhausted its second edition, tells about how the peoples of that continent live their lives. It covers their religion, politics, music, and, of course, their history.

As a child, Phyllis was wide-eyed with curiosity when returning Baptist missionaries from Africa told stories of exotic-sounding people and animals — "especially crocodiles." In high school, Phyllis planned to be a teacher. She collected stamps from the missionaries, still hoping that she would someday go to Africa. She liked the two courses she had in African history at Edinburgh University. Then she went on to Oxford for a year, received her teaching certificate, and taught for two years in high school at Guildford, in the county of Surrey, thirty miles from London.

The chance to go to Africa came when she saw an ad for a high school teacher in Ghana, applied for the job, and was hired to teach at Aburi Girls' Secondary School, located twenty miles from the capital city, Accra. She stayed for three years. In her youthful enthusiasm to see Africa she once hitch-hiked from Johannesburg in the extreme south of the continent to Cairo in the north. Since those early years of teaching, she has been back to Central Africa three times — to Angola, Zaire, and Congo — for research. In all, she has worked or traveled in about twenty African countries.

During those three years in Ghana important changes took place in Phyllis's life: she met Bradford Martin, the man whom she later married; she decided she wanted to do research and become a university professor; and she attended her first Friends meeting.

Hillhouse Friends Meeting is on the campus of the University of Ghana, near Accra. It was a silent meeting of about twenty or thirty people, mostly white expatriates. We asked Phyllis how she happened to go to the meeting. She said it took place on the first Sunday she was in Ghana when a faculty member at the school, who was looking after her as a newcomer, invited her to go.

"Do you go to church?" the woman asked.

"Yes, sometimes to Baptist or Presbyterian."

"I'm a Quaker and I go to Friends Meeting. Would you like to come with me?"

"I'm in a strange country doing strange things. Why not?"

It turned out not to be strange, though. She felt comfortable and she said, "I knew immediately that this was where I wanted to stay." She said she had already been moving away from the Protestant mainstream, beginning as early as her undergraduate years when she came under the influence of the more liberal approach of the Student Christian Movement. "At Edinburgh and Oxford I was more interested in the meditative aspects of religion," she said. Meditation in an old abbey, on the island of Iona off the west coast of Scotland, was a new and meaningful experience. This took place during work camps when students helped to rebuild the abbey. At Oxford, she attended High Anglican evensong services in New College chapel. Following her three years in Ghana, she enrolled at London University for graduate studies, finding time to attend Friends meetings for worship during two years of study there. Likewise, during six months in The Hague in Holland, and again for a several months in Paris, she found Friends meetings. She felt drawn to Quakerism by the silent meetings for worship, she said. In the beginning, she was not so familiar with Quaker social action.

Phyllis came to Bloomington and our Friends meeting in 1968. She was by then married to Bradford Martin, a member of the history department faculty at Indiana University. She recalls that her first Sunday at meeting for worship here, in October 1968, was also the first meeting held in the new meeting room addition. She became a member in 1972.

The late 1960s and 1970s were years of change, as Phyllis began life in a foreign country as a faculty wife and the mother of two children, Jennifer (Jenny) and Philip. She completed her dissertation and received her doctorate from London University in 1970. She began teaching part-time in the history department at Indiana University in 1972 and received a full-time appointment nine years later.

In 1979 Phyllis was divorced and became a single parent. Both children are now in college. Jenny is a senior at Ball State University in Muncie, Indiana, and Philip is a sophomore at Macalester College in St. Paul, Minnesota. Jenny was born with spina bifida and has undergone surgery many times. She now drives a car especially equipped for a handicapped person. While in high school Philip delivered newspapers, and during a six-week stay at home between semesters at midyear just past, he had a job to help with his expenses. Friends who knew Jenny and Philip as children and young teens in the Meeting feel a fond sense of pride in their developing independence.

Extraordinary family responsibilities, combined with a career in teaching and scholarship, have not kept Phyllis from work on behalf of our meeting. On the contrary, she has served on every committee, has been clerk of several, and was clerk of the monthly meeting for four years. She is currently clerk of both the Nominating and the Social committees. She is also a member of the Board on Peace and Christian Social Concerns of Western Yearly Meeting and is the Yearly Meeting representative to the Corporation (the legal governing body) of the American Friends Service Committee. In 1982 she represented Western Yearly Meeting on the Friends World Committee for Consultation and attended the Triennial Meeting at Kaimosi, in western Kenya, East Africa.

Phyllis is sensitive to the needs of our meeting and of individual Friends, recognizing differences while at the same time remaining true to her own religious orientation. As an undergraduate, she was influenced by Paul Tournier, a Christian Swiss psychologist whose writings seem to parallel the Quaker doctrine of the Inner Light and its effect in relation to other people. She mentioned her appreciation for Harold Loukes, a teacher whom she admired at Oxford University without knowing until later that he was a Quaker. More recently, she has been interested in Elizabeth Watson's writings on Quaker women and on women in the Gospels. A liberating force is her acquaintance with African religions and the realization that their beliefs are only a different way of answering the same ultimate questions shared by all of us.

While working within Western Yearly Meeting in Friends United Meeting, Phyllis has taken time to attend Ohio Valley Yearly Meeting, and last summer she attended the annual gathering of Friends General Conference held in the North Carolina mountains. "I am not sure that the true consensus of our Meeting is any longer accommodated by being only in Western Yearly Meeting," she said. "I have a strong sense that our Meeting is a bridge between conservative Friends and liberal Friends. My own orientation is more to the East Coast and European tradition, but living in the Midwest and being part of Western Yearly Meeting has enriched my experience as a Quaker. I feel an obligation to try and be a loyal member of the local Meeting, wherever I happen to live. My concern is the well-being of our Meeting, and I think this can only be achieved when we truly listen to each other."

Whether teaching a class, attending a committee meeting, or managing a Christmas potluck dinner at the meeting-house, Phyllis has the ability to focus her full energies on whatever task is at hand. She finds time to open the door of her home to foreigners in Bloomington during holidays, when they might be lonely. Recently, she has started working with the local hospice organization. The cosmopolitan Baptist-turned-Quaker says: "What I got from my father was important. He related not only to God, but to people."

— Judy Edgerton, March 1992

QUAKER PROFILE No. 24:

Warren Prentice Henegar

As a slender youth of sixteen who falsified his birth certificate in order to be accepted into the Navy, Warren Henegar grew to his full height of six feet two inches and established a view of the world's problems and how he might face them while he was aboard a Navy destroyer in the Pacific during World War II. Warren speaks of himself as having been "radicalized" by his wartime experiences. In June 1941, when Russia became an ally in the war against Nazi Germany, the thoughtful teenage boy recalled how less than two years earlier Russia had invaded Finland and how he had strongly sympathized with the Finns. He was likewise disturbed after Pearl Harbor, when West Coast hysteria led our government to put American citizens of Japanese ancestry into internment camps.

Today Warren maintains a natural skepticism that forces him to examine popular opinion, to inform himself, and to draw his own conclusions. The term "socially conscious" seems to describe him more aptly than his own word "radicalized". This was confirmed in 1978 when the Indiana Council of Churches named him Layman of the Year for his work with social service organizations.

Warren's father, William Walker Henegar, was killed in a construction accident when Warren was four and a half years old. His mother, Venera Beatrice Tays Henegar, pregnant with her sixth child, tried to keep the family going as tenant farmers with the help of her five children — there were two sons and a daughter older than Warren, and one son younger.

The baby girl born after their father's death died of diphtheria at the age of eighteen months.

The Henegars lived on the southern high plains in west Texas, in what is known as the last frontier. The territory had been occupied by the fierce horsemen of the Comanche tribe of Indians, who lived mainly in Texas until the Medicine Lodge Treaty of 1867 pushed them and their allies, the Kiowa and the Kiowa Apaches, into southwestern Oklahoma, where they struggled against white encroachment and remained. (Over four thousand Comanches now live scattered in Oklahoma.) Until the 1930s, the high plains in Texas consisted of rich farmland located on a plateau 3,500 feet high, an area that was being resettled by people other than the Indians as late as the 1920s. On the farm where Warren's family lived, he remembers fruit trees, grape vines, and the staple crop, cotton.

Tragedy struck that whole plains area in 1934 and 1935 — a catastrophe that Warren says was the equal of the pestilences, the acts of nature, described in the Old Testament. Severe drought turned the fertile land into blowing dust, blinding anything living in the path of windstorms. Little vegetation was left; and people, wildlife, and domestic livestock weakened and died. The area became known as the Dust Bowl, and the devastation is recorded in history textbooks and in such novels as John Steinbeck's *Grapes of Wrath*. Even before the Dust Bowl, the Great Depression had taken its toll in Texas, as elsewhere. Warren's fatherless family moved to a small town, Levelland, and then to Littlefield. As a school-age child, he carried his share of the load in keeping the family going, taking odd jobs — he called it "hustling" — and buying food for the family with his earnings. During some of that time a farmer, whose name was John I. Boling, gave Warren work and took the half-orphan under his wing. This man lived his religion, Warren said, and had a strong influence on him.

Warren gives much credit to the strength and optimism of his mother. Her own education stopped before high school, but she was self-taught and capable, challenging her five children to become well educated. Warren read widely even before his teen years. He demonstrated his precociousness after the war by passing the necessary tests for college entrance without having graduated from high school.

Along with thousands of other returning veterans, Warren went to college with financial help from the government through what was known as the G.I. Bill, first entering Texas Technological University in Lubbock in 1947. He spent his junior year at Stanford University and graduated with a bachelor's degree in English and history from Oklahoma City University in 1951.

He got employment with the U.S. Social Security Administration in San Francisco, where he met JoAnna Nix at a Civil Rights Congress rally. Their first acquaintance with the Society of Friends came after their marriage and their move to Eugene, Oregon. [More details can be found in Profile No. 21 for JoAnna, earlier in this book.] Warren said he was first attracted to the Society of Friends because it appeared to be unafraid to take a stand on unpopular issues, without regard to fashionable trends or mainstream appearances. "The only people standing up to the witch-hunting during the dark days of McCarthyism in 1951 and 1952 were a few ministers — and the Quakers," Warren said. He recalled that our country had stopped shipping food and medicine to Russia (devastated by World War II), and the Quakers kept on sending aid. He added that because of their unpopular disagreement with what was going on, he and JoAnna needed "a refuge of like-minded people," and Friends provided them with that support.

In 1955 the Henegars moved to Bakersfield, California, and then to the headquarters for Social Security in Baltimore, Maryland. They came to Bloomington and bought their farm in 1957, as described in JoAnna's profile, when daughters Lillian, Anna, and Alice were at toddler and baby stages. Jane was born three years later. The young family was welcomed into the Bloomington meeting, and both parents became actively involved.

At home on his farm just south of Bloomington, Warren demonstrates that his favorite area of work is in the field of agronomy. In addition to the farm chores, Warren continues his outside professional life and is at the same time a politician and an activist for causes he believes in. In 1963, he took a job offered by the Federal Soil Conservation Service in the local Soil and Water Conservation District (SWCD) serving Brown and Monroe counties. He has served on the board of the SWCD for many years. During a year's leave of absence in 1969, he obtained a master's degree in agronomy from Purdue University and subsequently became an adviser to farmers for the Monroe County Farm Bureau. He is now an environmental specialist with the Monroe County Health Department. This work involves advising and designing on-site waste-water and septic systems.

Both his social-service activities and his political offices are the result of his concerns as a Quaker. He believes that Quakers have an obligation to share in the responsibility for the best possible government for themselves, their families, and their neighbors by holding public office for at least two terms — provided they do not have to neglect their families and they have the personality to be effective. In 1970, he was elected to the Monroe county council, his first political office, which he held until 1976. He is at present on the county council and on the county planning commission. He ran for Congress in 1972 as a McGovern Democrat. He was a county commissioner from 1976 to 1984 and was president of the commission for several years.

Elected officials can point to new streets, public buildings, and even war memorial statues among their accomplishments; but Warren played a unique role in the erection of a monument to peace, which stands on the Monroe County courthouse lawn. Howard Canada, well-known for his public service in Bloomington, has written a short history of the peace statue. He says that in 1978 the county received some funds for job training from the federal government's Comprehensive Employment and Training Act (CETA). "County Commissioners determined that an appropriate area for training would be stonecutting. [Commissioners] Warren Henegar and John Irvine were assigned responsibility for implementing the program." William Dahman, then studying human anatomy at Indiana University as part of his job training as a stonecutter, was given a grant to produce a statue. He wanted to make one dedicated to peace. "Mr. Henegar agreed that the courthouse lawn should have a statue dedicated to peace to promote the fact that there is an alternative to war as a means of handling relations and settling disputes between nations." Warren, with the support of John Irvine, persuaded the other commissioners to have the peace statue carved and added to the war memorials already there. The figure of a woman holding aloft a dove of peace was dedicated by Warren himself on May 30, 1979. Some years later, when our local Congregations for Peace discovered that the hand holding the dove had broken off and disappeared, they undertook to have it restored. William Galloway, a talented stonecutter of Nashville, Indiana, volunteered to make the repairs at no cost, and on June 14, 1991, the newly restored statue to peace was rededicated in an impressive ceremony that included Howard Canada's history, from which this account is taken.

For some ten years in the 1970s and 1980s, Warren was a member of the board of Bread for the World, an ecumenical movement started by Arthur Simon, a Lutheran, and then joined by Catholics as well as other Protestant groups. He also served for eight years on the board of another nationwide Christian organization, Alternatives, dealing with the destruction of the environment and the perverting by commercialization of the church's holy celebrations, Christmas and Easter. He was featured in a United Methodist film posing the question, "How do we live in a hungry world?" Among the several local organizations that have used his services on their boards are the South Central Community Action Program and the Mental Health Association of Monroe County.

As a result of his broad contacts outside Bloomington Friends Meeting in areas of political and social action, Warren's contributions in our meetings for worship and for business are all the more valuable. He maintains the habit established in early youth of informing himself in depth, a case in point being the local debate over the proper disposal of polychlorinated biphenyls (PCBs) that have been dumped at various sites in Monroe County.

Warren says the writings of Howard Brinton have increased his understanding of Quakerism. As a young boy he liked the works of Charles Dickens. Later Tolstoy's *War and Peace* had a profound effect on his thinking. His brothers no longer belong to the Methodist church, the family's denomination while Warren was growing up, but they and his sister take their chosen religious affiliations seriously. His mother died in 1969.

Warren told us on March seventh that he has already planted five vegetables in his garden, turning the soil by hand because he likes to do it that way. He is an avid gardener. His farm acreage on South McCormick Road is in woods and in pasture for his herd of beef cattle, his four Thoroughbred horses, and his one small donkey, kept so that his six grandchildren can learn to ride safely. The contrast that quietly tending his garden and his animals offers to the outside demands of professional and political careers as well as social activism has no doubt helped to create the balanced, unflappable Quaker, Warren Henegar.

— Judy Edgerton, April 1992

QUAKER PROFILE No. 25:

James Tyler Nichols

During the years from 1961 to 1973, when the United States participated in the war between North and South Vietnam, a whole generation of our country's youth was forced into an abrupt halt in normal expectations for their lives. Questions of the morality of war were brought into focus for more people of all ages than at any previous time. For Jim Nichols, it was a time of decision about taking a stand as a conscientious objector to war, a decision made after much thought and preparation, and based on an upbringing where Christian principles are an important way of life.

Jim's stand as a conscientious objector, when facing draft registration in his teens, was made largely with the guidance of religious leaders in the Methodist church. As early as age fifteen, he was influenced by articles on pacifism in *Together*, the Methodist magazine for families. The large church in Bartlesville, Oklahoma, where he grew up, had always been supportive of its small numbers of pacifists, Jim said, adding that there have been pacifists in the Methodist church as far back as the French and Indian Wars in the eighteenth century. In addition to receiving counsel from individuals, including Quakers, he received practical information from a packet of articles and pamphlets put together by the National Interreligious Service Board for Conscientious Objectors. He also attended conferences for missionaries at DePauw University in Greencastle, Indiana, a Methodist institution. The missionaries he met were on furlough from their posts and had strong concerns about the Vietnam War. In addition to his convictions about the deliberate sacrifice of human life in war, he felt the weight of the deaths in Vietnam to such an extent that he had a vision of a burden placed on him. He made his definite decision as a part of the Methodist Youth Program in 1967. At age eighteen he registered with his draft board as a C.O., determined never to be a part of the armed services regardless of any consequences for him. The draft board had an attorney who met with conscientious objectors, advising them about the possible consequences of their choice. Alternative service of various kinds was allowed. Those who chose not even to register were sent to prison, while still others fled the country.

Jim had student deferment for the last year of high school and again as a student at Oklahoma City University, where he enrolled as a freshman. In college he found a network of other Methodists of his age group who were of the same mind. His own draft number was never called up, but he remained outspoken in his convictions, speaking to groups and talking to individuals one on one, sometimes changing minds. He is acquainted with C.O.'s who were assigned to alternative service such as work in hospitals, and with some who went to prison.

Thus the Quaker peace testimony was already well illustrated in Jim's life before he became a Friend. "Pappy Cash taught me how to be a Quaker long before I became a Quaker," he said. The man called Pappy was his maternal grandfather, a Methodist minister. Two uncles and an older brother are also Methodist ministers. The brother, like Jim, is a C.O. Jim spent summer vacation time with his Cash grandparents while growing up, and corresponded with Pappy while in college. Jim's mother, Elizabeth Cash Nichols, was not entirely sure how her father would react when she told him about his two grandsons' decisions to be conscientious objectors, because two of his sons had been in the armed forces in World War II. But Pappy simply said, "I don't blame them." Having lived near military bases, he said he had always had moral problems with the military lifestyle and the immorality behind it. Jim said his grandfather was open to the leading of the Holy Spirit, and quoted him as saying about the revelation of religious truth: "When the cup overflows, that means nobody owns it."

James Hugh Nichols, Jim's father, and his mother were deeply involved in the work of the Methodist church. He describes their home life as having had a pietistic atmosphere, in which self-discipline was important. It was understood that smoking, drinking, and gambling were unacceptable. A passage of scripture was read at the evening meal. His father was an engineer with the Phillips Petroleum Company and spent much of his career in England after Jim was in college. He had been an army officer in World War II, and said to his family afterward that there had to be a better way of dealing with problems in the world. He and Jim's mother are now retired and live in Atlanta, Georgia.

The family home in Bartlesville, Oklahoma, was across the street from a pastoral Friends Meeting, one that practiced some silence. Jim was acquainted with the work of Hominy Center Friends' Indian Program. His first association with Friends worship was at the unprogrammed Oklahoma City Friends Meeting while he was a graduate student at the University of Oklahoma. He and Sandra Key Wolf, also a graduate student, attended that Meeting together and were married under its care in 1975. They are now sojourners in our Bloomington Meeting from the Campus Friends Meeting at Wilmington College, in Ohio.

The combination of a religious upbringing, a mystical approach to religion, and the pacifist stance have made the transition to Quakerism seem natural. Jim said he thinks of himself as "a Christ-centered Friend, not in terms of words, but in terms of spiritual reality. I think if you center your life day-to-day in the leadings of the Christ spirit, then you are Christ-centered. It has nothing to do with language."

Following graduate studies at the University of Oklahoma, Jim studied at the University of Denver. He has also taught at Otero Junior College and worked at the University of Colorado library. From 1982 to 1985, he was public services librarian at Indiana University East in Richmond, Indiana, where the Nicholses were members of Clear Creek Meeting on the Earlham College campus. Then he was library director at Wilmington College in Ohio for six years before the family's move to Bloomington. He is now a doctoral candidate in library and information science at Indiana University. He and Sandy and their sons James, age twelve, and Andrew, age seven, came to Bloomington in August 1991. In addition to his course work at Indiana University, Jim is employed part time in the Lilly Library, and has also been teaching a course entitled Academic Libraries during this semester. "I have seen my vocation to be that of a teacher," he said. "As a librarian, I teach individuals. Any teaching can be a ministry.

"I have been involved in the Friends Association for Higher Education, attending annual sessions at Wilmington College and at Swarthmore College in Pennsylvania," he continued. "The meetings are open, with a program lasting five or six days. Quaker faculty from non-Quaker institutions also attend. My special interest at these meetings was in the Committee of Quaker Studies for Human Betterment. I find it is strengthening to meet Friends from various places on a spiritual level."

Jim is familiar with the history of the Society of Friends through his reading. He mentioned in particular the journals of George Fox and John Woolman. He is well grounded in the Bible and he knows present-day Quakerism through active participation. He was clerk of Campus Friends Meeting at Wilmington College at the time they left for Bloomington. He had also been the recording clerk and a member of Ministry and Counsel. He was the recording clerk of Ohio Valley Yearly Meeting for three years. He served on the Junior Yearly Meeting Committee and was on the board of the Dayton branch of the American Friends Service Committee. He served as recording clerk and edited the proceedings for the Quaker Studies for Human Betterment Committee in 1989. He did some counseling of young pacifists of draft age while he was at Clear Creek Meeting in Richmond.

Jim's heavy schedule at the university makes it difficult for him to spend much time nowadays with his family. Sandy says, "The boys miss him." He arranges his schedule so as always to be with his family on Friday evenings. They feel it is important to attend Friends meeting together on Sunday mornings. He describes the Wilmington Friends Meeting as older and more settled than our Bloomington Meeting and says that it has fewer families with children, fewer attenders, and there is more speaking out of the silence in meetings for worship.

Friends from a wide variety of experiences, as members or attenders, provide a leavening agent that we value in our Bloomington Meeting. Repeating the last sentence of Sandy's profile earlier in this book: We claim the Nichols family joyfully and hope they will stay for a very long time.

— Judy Edgerton, May 1992

QUAKER PROFILE No. 26:

James Jay Morgan

James Morgan is a convinced Friend. He was a sojourner at Homewood Meeting in Baltimore and still belongs to Mountain View Friends Meeting in Denver, Colorado. He grew up in the British colony of the Bermuda Islands, located in the Atlantic Ocean six hundred miles east of Cape Hatteras, North Carolina. The family home was on St. George's Island, the second largest after Bermuda Island, and connected to it by a bridge. His father, William Morgan, was a civilian employee at the United States military base. Jim's parents were Lutheran, but there was no Lutheran church in Bermuda. His father took Jim and the other three children to various Sunday services. His mother's name is Audrey Selle Morgan. The Morgans had two daughters and another son, all younger than Jim.

The total area of the islands is twenty square miles, connected by bridges and ferries. Jim says the entire land area is comparable to that of Bloomington. The main source of revenue is tourism. For many years no cars were allowed on the island — only horse-drawn vehicles. At one time there was a train, but it was later replaced by a bus system. Cars arrived for the first time in 1946. The speed limit is still twenty miles per hour. When Jim was there, the population was around forty thousand, but he says it is now over fifty thousand. Although half the population of Bermuda is of African ancestry, the small British-type school of 150 pupils that Jim attended from 1950 to 1959 was for white and mulatto children, and his teachers were either English or Scottish. Jim was a voracious reader, quiet but with wide-ranging interests, and ahead of his age group. While growing up, he read everything written by the prolific English writer of books for young people, Enid Blyton. The study of French began in the fourth year. Pupils in the second through the fourth form were in the same room. A certain code of behavior was taken for granted, he said, and there were few disciplinary problems. He attributes his sense of values, and the comfortable feeling he has in Quaker circles, to his early training in that school.

He contrasts the underlying philosophy of his British schooling to that of the Lutheran parochial school (Missouri Synod) where he spent his last year of high school in Milwaukee, Wisconsin. In his first nine years, the emphasis was on responsibility and service, while the emphasis in the parochial school was on "faith rather than works," just as it was at Valparaiso University, which he entered after high school graduation. At Valparaiso, Jim had two years of religious training. In his freshman year he wrote a weekly essay on the epistle of the week. In his sophomore year, he studied the Old Testament and wrote a term paper on the religious philosopher Kierkegaard. Included in the course was the study of the Egyptian psalms: hymns of praise and hymns to the sun god. He graduated from Valparaiso with a double major in French and government.

In 1967, Jim interrupted graduate study at the University of Denver and joined the Peace Corps. He was assigned to teach English as a foreign language in Ivory Coast, West Africa, where French was the national language. He was located in the city of Korhogo, in the Savannah region.

When his two years in the Peace Corps were up in 1969, he resumed his graduate work at the University of Denver. It was then that he decided to find out about the Quakers and attended Mountain View Friends Meeting for the first time. He looks back with amusement now on his first visit, when he sat quietly for a whole hour of silence while he waited for something to happen. Suddenly everyone around him was shaking hands, including Jim himself. He said that a meeting member, Barney Aldrich, introduced himself after the meeting and told him what had been going on. Leonore Goodenow, the meetinghouse resident and caretaker, tutored him in the Quaker manner of worship, and gave him advice about reading material. He spoke with appreciation of the annual gathering of the Intermountain Faith Fellowship (now Intermountain Yearly Meeting), of which Mountain View was a part. As a newcomer to Quakerism, Jim was strengthened by the example of an elderly Friend he met at the Faith Fellowship, Gordon Graves. Together with other Friends, Gordon Graves had begun a peace vigil on a Denver street corner during the Vietnam War. A man past eighty years of age and leaning on a cane, he kept up the vigil year after year while Jim was in Denver.

In 1971 Jim moved to Baltimore, where he was employed by the Social Security Administration. There he became a sojourning member of the Homewood Monthly Meeting, and there he met Laurel Cornell, a birthright Friend, who was then a doctoral candidate at Johns Hopkins University. They were married under the care of Homewood Meeting in 1973. Jim says he is indebted to the very good collection of books in Homewood Meeting for his background reading in Quaker literature. He mentioned *Friends for 300 Years* by Howard Brinton, *Meetinghouse and Counting House* by Frederick Tolles, *The History of the Life of Thomas Ellwood*, which is an autobiography by a contemporary of George Fox, and Jan de Hartog's novel *The Peaceable Kingdom.*

After Laurel completed her residence work at Johns Hopkins, they moved to Philadelphia, where Jim worked for a biological indexing and abstracting firm while taking a master's degree in Library and Information Science at Drexel University. They attended several of the Friends meetings in the Philadelphia area during those years. In 1983, they moved to Ithaca, New York, where Laurel was appointed to teach at Cornell University and Jim became a library automation consultant for a regional library organization covering seventeen counties. His work ranged over an area the size of Indiana and included the libraries of schools, hospitals, and industrial companies among its eighty members.

Jim and his family came to Bloomington in 1987. Laurel joined the faculty of Indiana University as a member of the Sociology department, and Jim became automation librarian in the Ruth Lilly Medical Library at the Indiana University

School of Medicine in Indianapolis. Jim says the facility is new and well-arranged, and he enjoys being there.

Since he began attending our Bloomington Meeting, we have benefited from his skill in working with young people, from toddlers through high school. He is now taking a turn as clerk of the Maintenance committee. As a librarian, he highly recommends the Monroe County Public Library to parents for their children's reading. As time allows, Jim still reads for pleasure. Since Laurel introduced him to English and contra dancing, this has become an important form of relaxation from the responsibilities and service so important in his life.

When we first talked with Jim over dinner on July twenty-fourth, he was looking forward to a trip two weeks later to Japan. The first time Laurel and Jim were in Japan, in 1979–80, they lived in the Japanese "Alps" in a small town, Chino, located near Lake Suwa. At that time Laurel was gathering data for her doctoral dissertation, while Jim worked part-time as a librarian at Sophia University and enjoyed observing the mountain scenery and people from the vantage point of a bicycle.

Jim's plan was to leave for Kyoto on August eighth, to join Laurel and their eight-year-old son Morris, who have been there for four months. Laurel is doing further research in her field, sociology. Jim went with them to Kyoto last March and stayed for a month, helping to enroll Morris in a Japanese school before returning to Bloomington. Now Jim will get the chance to meet the friends Morris has made in Kyoto. After a short stay, he plans to bring Morris back to Bloomington in time for the opening of school here; Laurel will follow her family a week later, after winding up her six months of research.

* * *

It is now September, two months since we first talked with Jim. The Cornell and Morgan family is back in Bloomington. During the time Morris spent with Laurel in Japan, he had the opportunity to get to know the families of his Japanese classmates, who invited him to their birthday parties and took him with them to special events, such as festivals. He did a lot of bicycling with his closest friend, and they enjoyed walking the dog. "Children have a way of communicating without the language," Jim said. In return, Morris enjoyed having one of his friends go with his family as they visited the Youth Science Center, a wild-monkey park, and took a trip to the seaport of Kobe. Morris's teacher explained regular assignments to him in English, so he had a very good school experience, learning along with his classmates. He especially enjoyed learning to read the "do, re, mi" musical notes. The teacher gave him the musical instrument he used in class, a combined wind and keyboard instrument.

A part of the curriculum would seem to be the teaching of responsibility. Each morning, all the students gathered in small groups in local parks and walked to school together, with an older student leading. Then they played unsupervised in their classrooms until the teacher arrived. Morris liked helping to prepare the food and bring it out to serve at lunch, and helping with classroom cleanup.

Now home again, Morris is enrolled in the third grade at University Elementary School. Welcome home, Morris, Laurel, and Jim!

— Judy Edgerton, September 1992

QUAKER PROFILE No. 27:

Jonathan Frederick Anderson

No solemn-faced Quaker, Jonathan Anderson's infectious laugh tells any gathering that here is an example of the phrase *joie de vivre*. With his rich natural voice, sometimes accompanied by the guitar, he is a kind of beneficent Pied Piper to both children and adults, leading them to "make a joyful noise" in song.

Jonathan is equally comfortable, whether coaching young children on their level to an awakening of religious insight, or assuming a quiet role in the process of consensus in Quaker meeting for business. Both of these abilities are rooted in his devotion to his own family and his belief in the Christian way of life. "Two things are important in my life," he says. "They are God and family." He has always sought to know God's will ("What does the Lord require of thee?"), and he is devoted heart and soul to the welfare and future of his family. In the first instance, he finds it frustrating when he cannot be entirely sure of the answer to the biblical question concerning God's will. In the second instance, his three well-adjusted children — two teenage daughters and a twelve-year-old son — attest to the wisdom of his choice in placing family values uppermost. He decries co-opting that phrase for political use, linking it up with such things as capital punishment and the subordination of women, which makes a mockery of what he understands as family values — love, caring, sensitivity, and responsibility.

When he declares that he believes in the good news of Jesus Christ, Jonathan does not mean he is a fundamentalist in the rigid sense associated with that word. Rather, he interprets what he describes as a very radical Christianity to be not only a religion but a way of life, grounded in love, mercy, and forgiveness, which he understands to be at the root of Quaker beliefs. This way of life takes form through one's own relationship with the spirit of God. He feels strongly that a window to understanding is provided by love as interpreted in the life of Christ. Although this is not the only way, he says, it is the one by which he is guided.

Concerning his own three children, Emily Michelle, Alicia April Joy (Tia), and Justin Gordon Frederick, Jonathan said he very much enjoyed the closeness established when he took over the role of primary care-giver. His wife, Mary Patricia Goodman Anderson, felt gratified and fulfilled in that role when the children were infants and toddlers, but she gave it over to Jonathan when she started working for a college degree at Montana State University in Bozeman, in 1984. During one whole year Jonathan taught their children by the home-school method. He himself got a great deal from reading children's literary classics aloud — things he said he had largely missed as he was growing up. The children loved it, and loved hearing him sing to them and play the guitar. Now that they are older, he likes following their interests as he takes them to their various activities outside home and school. "Children are really no different from me," he says. "I treat them as people, and they know that quickly. They are not in the way — not an inconvenience — they are enjoyable people. I relate to kids."

The second visible witness to his Christian — and Quaker — principles, his C.O. status, had its roots in his early youth. He grew up knowing the Bible well from regular attendance at church and Sunday school, first as a grade-school child at an American Baptist church in Evanston, Illinois, and later in a socially active church, United Presbyterian, in Rockville, Maryland, throughout his high school years. Jesus' teachings such as "Thou shalt not kill," "Love thy neighbor," and "Turn the other cheek" — all pacifist concepts — made a lasting impression. His mother, Carol Annie White Anderson, was an example for him in that she was, and still remains, actively engaged in social service and church-related activities. His father, Gordon Frederick Anderson, had less time for working outside of the heavy responsibilities he carried in his profession as public school administrator, both in Illinois and in Maryland.

Jonathan's first contact with Quakers was at age sixteen, when he went to Mexico with a Quaker youth group and helped with some work-camp projects there, along with sightseeing. The Anderson home in Rockville, Maryland, was near enough to Washington, D.C., for members of his Presbyterian Church youth group to take part in the civil rights marches in Washington in the late 1960s. He was participating in the Poor People's Campaign at the time Martin Luther King was assassinated in 1968. The subsequent rioting and property damage, including devastating fires in Washington, resulted in consciousness-raising in civil rights for young Jonathan.

In 1969 Jonathan enrolled at Colorado State University with the goal of becoming a forest ranger. That year was a frustrating time for the seventeen-year-old freshman. First of all, he was unprepared, especially for the math and chemistry required for a degree in his chosen course of study. High school academic preparation had been sacrificed for other activities: work to become an Eagle Scout and participation in almost all the sports programs as well as in the school's singing groups. An even greater problem for him that year, as well as for every young person in his age category, was the Vietnam War. He was brought face to face with the dilemma that he might be drafted for military service when it was his conviction that he could not kill. Self-doubt caused him to wonder whether he was only being cowardly when he registered as a conscientious objector at the end of that freshman year. By the beginning of the fall semester of his second year, he had not heard from his draft board. Feeling that he might still be drafted, in which case he would no longer be in control of his life, he took a drastic step and enlisted in the Army as a medical noncombatant. He remembers how his mother caught her breath when he telephoned her from Colorado to say he had joined the Army. She turned the phone over to his father, who listened and talked with him about the decision.

He trained at Fort Knox, Kentucky, and Fort Sam Houston, Texas, and he was at Fort Benning, Georgia, for three weeks of parachute school. Doubts continued to plague him, causing second thoughts about his choice to be a part of "support troops" as a medic, because that role was, he said, "after all, just that: support in order to kill." He learned that there was a way to apply for C.O. status while in the Army, so he started the application process. He was then posted to the Walter Reed Hospital in Washington, D.C., and felt it was fortunate that his application went through medical personnel, making the process easier. He said he believed his application was given more favorable treatment because his reasoning was based on religion and a belief in Jesus Christ. He was granted an honorable discharge in 1971.

Back at Colorado State, he began a major in political science, changed to history, and then graduated in December 1974 with teacher certification and a B.A. in history. The experience he had as a practice teacher, dealing with rebellious high school students who were unwilling to learn, convinced him that he did not want to teach. A notable exception was one very bright and attractive young senior girl, Mary Patricia Goodman, who was expecting to graduate from high school in December at the same time as his graduation from college. The attraction he felt for Mary Goodman was returned. They dated after her course work was finished, and they were married in an outdoor setting on a hillside at sunrise on June 22, 1975. Mary wore a white gown and Jonathan wore a white surplice, both with embroidery on the front done by the bride. The couple wrote their own ceremony, "marrying each other before God." Included in the service were readings and singing by members of the family. So with their families and some friends in attendance, they said their vows to each other without knowing that they were following a tradition of Friends, and they fulfilled the legal requirements by having the witness of a deacon from the Catholic church.

Jonathan described taking his bride to live in a primitive trailer without running water, where he worked as a farm hand. That summer, they left Colorado in a pickup truck, taking odd jobs before they both found work in Illinois in a factory making television parts. Their nomadic life ended after a few months when they were offered jobs at the large church in Evanston where Jonathan had been baptized as a child by the minister who still served there. They were given a joint appointment as youth counselors, and Jonathan also assumed the responsibilities of sexton. Their compensation was a stipend and the occupancy of a comfortable apartment in the church.

Following that pleasant experience, their lives took a very different turn. They traveled to Washington, where Jonathan took the Foreign Service examination and surprised himself by passing it. In Washington they took part in a learning experience in communal living that had a Christian base, while Jonathan worked as a hall monitor in a public high school — a highly objectionable job. Their first child, Emily, was born during that year. They moved in their second year into the very nice home of a retired Presbyterian minister in Bethesda, Maryland, in exchange for taking care of him. In 1977–78 Jonathan was enrolled at American University and received a master's degree in public administration. Jonathan describes the home birth during that year of their second child, Tia, as a beautiful experience.

In June 1979, Jonathan entered the State Department, and during the next two years the family experienced life in Bangladesh, in a very different culture even though they were somewhat isolated from it by their State Department status. Jonathan spent his first year there as visa officer and his second year as political reporter. Meanwhile, Mary worked as a volunteer with an organization taking care of orphans — a meaningful experience which she shared with Jonathan. In 1980, one of the infants captured her heart. She and Jonathan adopted him and he became their son Justin.

Mary learned firsthand of the work done by Mother Teresa in the slums of Bangladesh. Jonathan relates an episode where someone asked Mother Teresa, "What is the purpose of helping people who will die anyway?" Her answer was, "God doesn't call me to be successful, but to be faithful" — a statement that he and Mary have taken to heart.

Their next assignment was to Australia. The year they spent there in 1981–82 seemed much like being in the United States. After their return home, Jonathan and the State Department were mutually dissatisfied, and he resigned his post. They received much needed support from Reston

Friends Preparatory Meeting, which they attended in Reston, Virginia.

Mary wanted very much to study for a degree in architecture, so she enrolled at Montana State University in Bozeman, where Jonathan found a job as manager of a taxicab company. Then he bought the company, enjoying the feeling of independence this gave him, especially the opportunity to participate in family life as he chose. Mary obtained her bachelor of architecture degree in 1989.

Now it was time for Jonathan to plan once again for the long-range future, and that is how he and his family moved to Bloomington. Indiana University offered the courses he wanted. Mary found a job in Bloomington, and the family moved here in 1989. Jonathan is now a candidate for the Ph.D. in public policy, jointly sponsored by the School of Public and Environmental Affairs and the Department of Political Science, concentrating on the resolution of ethnic conflicts. He has a part-time job with the Affirmative Action office at the university.

Mary and Jonathan had felt drawn to peace churches. They had worshipped with a group of Mennonites in Bangladesh, and had attended a Church of the Brethren in the Washington area. In 1989 when they came to Bloomington Friends Meeting, Jonathan said that they "discovered we had been Quakers all along. Everything strongly resonated with the convictions we had held all our lives: the peace testimony, silent worship with no minister, the ideals of consensus — these concepts had been in our minds for years, but there had never been a place where they all came together. We call ourselves very convinced Friends! We wanted to join not just the local monthly meeting but the larger Society of Friends. We are no longer church-shopping. We have definitely found our spiritual home. If we were in a place with no Friends meeting, we would start one." Mary and Jonathan became members of Bloomington Monthly Meeting and the Society of Friends in November 1990. In the short three years since they first came to us, both of them have contributed their energies in leadership roles with a kind of spiritual depth reminiscent of long-seasoned Friends.

— Judy Edgerton, October 1992

QUAKER PROFILE No. 28:

Joyce Adams

An in-depth conversation with Joyce Adams revealed a person of deep religious convictions, free of rigid dogmatism and exclusiveness. "All great religions are pointing to God," she has said. More than five years spent living in three foreign cultures undoubtedly gave her an understanding of the underlying religious philosophies of these countries — Germany, Bulgaria, and the countries of the former Soviet Union, including Central Asia. Bloomington Friends became acquainted with Joyce before her latest foreign sojourn, which was in Bulgaria in 1991–92. Before she left for Bulgaria she had attended our meeting a number of times, though she was living forty miles away in Terre Haute, where she was teaching at Rose Hulman Institute. While in Bulgaria she wrote to us, and after her return she began living in the Bloomington area. Recently, she purchased a home in nearby Ellettsville and has become a valued member of our meeting.

The person having the greatest influence on her religious development while she was growing up was her maternal grandmother, who "found joy in her spiritual life. She was filled with the Spirit in a quiet way." This grandmother had a thorough grounding in the Scriptures, having been trained at the Moody Bible Institute. Joyce described her mother, Caroline Lander Adams, as being a model of service and faithfulness as a member of the Presbyterian church. Although her father's association was with the more sectarian Church of the Brethren, his attitude was open and questioning. Both her father, Sidney Adams, and her mother encouraged Joyce in her own religious search. She appreciates having grown up in the kind of Presbyterian church that had a scholarly orientation. She regularly attended Sunday school and went to church camp in summers. Her parents were skeptical about the evangelical approach of the camp leaders. Its emphasis on self-denial created self-doubt and a feeling of guilt in their serious young daughter — a feeling of not being good enough as a Christian. A positive aspect of the camp was her first experience in getting to know African Americans as individuals, which marked the beginning of her social consciousness.

Joyce's schooling up to the time of college entrance was in the Arlington, Virginia, public schools. Her father had a doctorate in psychology with an emphasis on testing, and was engaged in work for the federal government in Washington. Her mother, with a Ph.D. in botany, was on the faculty of George Washington University.

Total immersion in a foreign culture began after Joyce's sophomore year at Oberlin College in Ohio. In 1958 she went to Germany to visit a high school friend, decided to enroll in Heidelberg University, and stayed on to earn a diploma in German language studies. Emerging with a fluency that approximates the bilingual skill of a person growing up with two languages, she decided upon a career in translation, which has more recently evolved into the teaching of English as a foreign language. Her Ph.D. is from the University of Chicago. She entered graduate school in 1961, completing her dissertation in 1968 while living in New Haven, Connecticut.

During her teaching of German to graduate students at Yale University in 1966–68, she took advantage of the opportunity to audit courses in the Russian language. In 1968–69, she accompanied her husband to the Soviet Union. He is a Canadian who was on the Yale faculty, and they were part of a Canadian exchange program with the Soviet Union. She describes the year spent in that closed society as one that surpassed all her previous experiences in the interesting contrasts it offered. The standard of living was in sharp contrast. All foreigners were housed together at Moscow State University, and although she learned on her own to converse with Russians, she was not allowed to take Russian language courses — possibly because the authorities feared contamination of the population by foreigners with democratic ideas. People she met as she went shopping or rode the subways were interested in learning about the West, and always expressed a desire for peace.

Back in New Haven, she continued to teach. At the same time, she took the chance to broaden her own education by translating articles from German on the subject of the Third Reich for a historian. In 1971, she and her husband adopted a son, Daniel, who at age two went with his parents for another stay of six months in the Soviet Union. So Joyce added to her previous experiences that of having her child in a Soviet nursery school, a feature of life in that country attracting much attention at the time in our news publications.

In 1974, Joyce left New Haven and settled with her husband and son in Davis, California. During the next four years she worked as a translator of German for a doctor of veterinary medicine, who was a Quaker. She was impressed by the spiritual energy of this man, attributing it to his Quakerism. Joyce had become an Episcopalian, which was her husband's faith.

After she was divorced in 1979, Joyce returned east to Washington, D.C. She found that Washington was permeated with a military atmosphere, something that was unsettling for her. She took refuge in Florida Avenue Friends Meeting. It was there that she came upon a book compiled by London Yearly Meeting that has meant a great deal to her. It consists of 670 short quotations from the writings of Quakers from the 1660s down to 1960, the date of its first publication. Its title is *Christian Faith and Practice in the Experience of the Society of Friends.*

Leaving Washington in March 1980, Joyce took a job in Ridgefield, Connecticut, as translator of German for a pharmaceutical company. Joyce describes herself as being at a low ebb, beginning in the mid-1980s when she felt that she should make a decision concerning her professional life. She went back to school, obtained a master's degree in applied linguistics, and took a teaching job. During that time she was concerned about her father, who was diagnosed as having Alzheimer's disease. He died in 1990. Responsibility as an only child weighs heavily, so now Joyce was involved in her mother's adjustment and change in living arrangements. In September of this year she helped her mother move to a comfortable retirement home in Alexandria, Virginia.

The year in Bulgaria, referred to earlier, was made possible by a Fulbright grant. Joyce taught English at the University of Plovdiv, where she was the only American in a town with a population of 450,000. She returned to Bloomington a year ago and is now teaching English composition at Indiana University-Purdue University Indianapolis, commuting twice each week for her classes. She is a member of the Midwest section of Teachers of English to Speakers of Other Languages, and on October 24, 1992, she gave a lecture in Indianapolis at a meeting of members from several states.

Joyce's first experience as an active participant in a Friends meeting was in Wilton, Connecticut, and later in Hartford. With the resumption of her teaching career and with roots now firmly established in this area, Joyce is becoming active in our meeting. She is a member of the Peace and Social Concerns committee and has served as acting recording clerk on several occasions in recent months.

Joyce longs for time for contemplation. She finds reading the Bible a source of strength, and she mentioned the writings of the monk Thomas Merton and the Dutch writer Henri Nouwen as being among her favorites. One would not guess from her friendly manner and open smile that she thinks of herself as a loner. She says she must be more willing to take risks in encounters with other people. "I start with the individual and his search for God and God's search for the person," she says. "The truth seems to lie in that relationship. Truth is experience; it is the process, not a statement." She was reminded of the poem "The Hound of Heaven," by the English poet Francis Thompson. The opening line is "I fled Him down the nights and down the days," and a line later on says, "Fear wist not to evade as Love wist to pursue." As a last thought she added: "Where love is, there is God."

— Judy Edgerton, November 1992

QUAKER PROFILE No. 29:

Teresa Kay Bohner Reynolds

Terry seemed somehow to be floating rather than walking into our house on the day we had our conversation about her religious journey. The word zephyr came to mind, something like a soft breeze from out of her home west of Bloomington, from out of a quiet place in the country where she and her family are nourished by nature in body and spirit. Along with greetings, there was an infectious laugh, announcing a vibrant personality. There is mature depth and inner strength about her, born of responsibility, initiative, and her share of pain. She has reached a firm conviction about the direction of her life, and has become a committed member of Bloomington Friends Meeting and the Society of Friends.

She did not try to explain how she seemed to be drawn toward the Friends meetinghouse as she passed it in her car every day on her way to and from work at Indiana University when she lived near Lake Monroe. In those days, she was undergoing a metamorphosis from the atheistic stance she had tried to take in conformity with the beliefs of her first husband and the father of her son, Caelum Roberts. They were divorced when Caelum was two years old. "I tried to deny my spiritual nature," she said. "It had to grow again. I overcame darkness outside me, and within."

Terry had once read a novel by the Quaker author Jessamyn West and said, "I knew only that Quakers were a peaceful people whose form of worship was in meditation." She felt an unexplainable tug, which was more than simple curiosity, to find out more sometime about the people who worshipped in the little house that she passed each day. The time finally arrived in 1981 when she took the step and came to meeting on a Sunday morning. Now, a decade later, after her marriage to Jerry Reynolds in 1982, she drives twenty miles from her home near Spencer every Sunday morning with her two daughters, Catherine (Kate), age seven, and Carrie, age five, and also with fifteen-year-old Caelum when he is not with his father. All three children became junior members when their mother made her decision to join our meeting.

Her husband, Jer, whom she describes as "creative," comes with her to special events at the meeting. He is a central stabilizing figure at home while Terry is away at work each day, since his office and workshop are in a separate building a few steps from their house. He is an engineer who designs and makes industrial controllers. Their house is an authentic, though new, log cabin, built by a master craftsman using original pioneer design with chinked logs. Jer quite literally "keeps the home fires burning" as he stokes the stove that is their main source of heat with wood from trees he has thinned out from their own forest.

Indeed, Terry, Jer, and their three children are closer to nature than most families are privileged to be in this industrialized and mechanistic age. While Jer is the wood-chopper and Terry is the chief gardener, the whole family shares in tasks like wood stacking and vegetable harvesting. Terry is an accomplished gardener — growing flowers in combination with vegetables, kneeling to plant in hundred-foot squares rather than in rows, and depending upon mulch rather than either cultivating or weeding. They eat from their garden beginning with greens in March or April and extending into late autumn. They fall asleep to soft night sounds from the meadows and woods — and sometimes get awakened by the long, eerie howls of coyotes that send their two large dogs scrambling under the porch in fear.

Terry grew up in a family where the daily transition from the fast-paced world of industry to an idyllic life at home was much like the life she has established with her own family. Her childhood home was eight miles from the nearest small town, Brookville, Indiana, thirty miles south of Richmond and not far from Cincinnati, Ohio, where the family often went on shopping trips. Terry's father, Charles Bohner, was employed by a branch of the Corning Glass Company in Brookville and her mother, Betty Howell Bohner, took a job with the same company after their daughters were in college. The Bohner home was nearly surrounded by a State tree farm. They had a lake of their own in front that was large enough for swimming, boating, and fishing.

Every child's dream of owning a pony came true for Terry at the age of eleven. She was sick in bed with flu when her parents brought the pony home as a surprise. She says she was instantly cured when she looked out her bedroom window and saw it. She ran outside and spent all afternoon riding her new pony, to which she gave the name Lucky.

Terry is very proud of her younger sister, Connie, who with the help of her family overcame major handicaps associated with her premature birth and is now an accomplished adult with an advanced academic degree. Terry recalls how the extended family of aunts, uncles, and young cousins would get together for overnights at various campsites, living in tents near some body of water, fishing, eating the catch, and enjoying each other's company.

While she was growing up, Terry spent much time out-of-doors. "I have had a wonderful life," she says. "I'm now building a lot, but in some ways I'm still coasting on childhood." Her mother was her chief religious influence, and nature nurtured that influence. "My mother is really a Quaker," she said, "but she doesn't know it! She is gentle and peaceful; she listens with an open mind, steps into the other person's shoes, sees that other point of view." Her parents did not attend any church, but started going to the small unaffiliated church in their rural community after Terry asked them to take her there. She had felt left out at school when the teacher asked the children each Monday morning, "Who went to church yesterday?" Terry said the only Sunday school material they had was the Bible itself. In summer, she was happy to see her school friends at a two-week vacation Bible school, and is still fond of the hymns she learned in those early years in that little country church.

Terry's parents went into early retirement when the local branch of the Corning Glass Company closed down, and they still live in their beautiful home, where Terry visits them when time allows. Her father had worked long hours away from home while she was growing up, but now she speaks warmly of her reacquaintance with him on an adult level, describing him as outgoing and personable. He volunteers when neighbors need help — for example, evacuating families from their homes when the Whitewater River occasionally overflows. Terry feels close to her parents and talks frequently with them by telephone.

Owing to her crowded schedule and the twenty-mile drive from her home, Terry regrets that she is not able to attend all of the extra affairs sponsored by the Meeting. But "meeting for worship is important," she says. "I need to be there. There is something about sitting in silence each Sunday, something that joins us to each other somehow. A community is there. Meeting gives me strength for the coming week. Sometimes I go off alone into the woods and spend an hour . . ." Her voice trails off, as though in thought. "I always wanted to be a teacher, and now I *am* a teacher." She has in mind her work with the First-day school, both teaching on Sundays and working in the Religious Education committee. She also has in mind her work at the School of Public and Environmental Affairs (SPEA). Her title is branch coordinator at the Business/SPEA library. A large part of her job is hiring and advising sixty work-study college students. She teaches them work habits and reassures them as they are about to graduate and look for jobs. They come to her with their problems when they need someone to talk to. A third and important part of her teaching, as with any mother, is the daily teaching of her own three children.

Terry is a regular member of the only worship-sharing group in the meeting. This now well-established group of around eight Friends gathers on Tuesday mornings in one of the rooms not in use at Terry's workplace in the SPEA building. One book in particular that the group has read and talked about was especially meaningful for her: *Original Blessing*, by Matthew Fox. In her own personal reading, she is partial to works concerning our relationship with nature, especially those by or about Native Americans. She herself has a great-grandfather who was from the Cherokee nation. Another responsibility she has at the Business/SPEA Library is for circulation and book reviews, with the help of three people on her staff. A by-product of this work is having ready access to books that fit her interest in nature and the environment. Her preferences in reading go back to her childhood, when she was a constant reader and when her favorite book of all was the famous dog story, *Lassie, Come Home.*

Terry holds fast to a thought that is said to be part of an Indian religious tradition: "I am at the center of everything. You, too, are the center of everything. To the east, west, north, and south — the sky above and the earth beneath — it all starts with me. I am God's guest, for it is His creation. I am here to care for it, to love, and to serve."

— Judy Edgerton, January 1993

QUAKER PROFILE No. 30:

Stephanie Shireman Boenau

(Pronounced Bay-no)

Stephanie knows why she is a Quaker. She would not say that Quakerism is the only way, or that any other approach to religion is wrong. She finds it strange that many religions proclaim their set of beliefs to be right and any other belief to be wrong. Rather, she thinks that religion is a search, and one's personal belief is not a place, but a path. "That," she says, "is why the concept of continuing revelation strikes such a chord with me."

Hers is a true religious journey, with mileposts along the way. She has memories from early childhood of being in the balcony of a large old church, looking down into the cavernous sanctuary to where the pulpit with a stair rose high above the congregation. She may not have understood the sermon, but she was so terrified by the minister's thunderous voice that when she saw him close up, she hid behind her Grandmother Harding.

Her maternal grandmother's devotion to a religious life made a profound impression on Stephanie. "Nana" felt closest to the United Church of Christ, but having an open mind she read literature from other religious groups, including some from her original Methodist background as well as from the Unity church and the Christian Scientists. She lived in the same town as Stephanie — Easton, Pennsylvania — and within walking distance, so her house was like another home.

Nana was a companion who taught her how to sew on her treadle machine and to play adult games, such as Scrabble.

After the death of the United Church of Christ minister, whom her parents (Woodrow E. and Faith Harding Shireman) considered to be charismatic, six-year-old Stephanie and her family left that downtown church and moved to the larger residential Presbyterian church near their home, in a section of Easton known as College Hill. They attended this church throughout her elementary years, and were involved with choir and a variety of other church-related activities up to the time that the political atmosphere created division and polarity among their friends. It was disturbing to her family that so many people from this church felt that the United States' involvement in Vietnam was correct. Also, while she especially appreciates what she learned there about the Bible, in looking back she feels that that church was not necessarily religious, especially in contrast to the depth of her grandmother's beliefs.

A pivotal point came at the age of twelve or thirteen, when her youth group was required to attend after-school classes in Presbyterian history and creed in preparation for confirmation. In discussions her friends appeared to believe that the war in Vietnam was correct, without having any reasons that seemed logical. She felt they did not know why they were joining the church, or what their religion meant to them. She herself did not feel she should accept that church at such a young age to the exclusion of other ways of thinking and worshiping, and now she believes that she was influenced by her grandmother's example of forming her own approach to God, based on her reading and personal experiences. What finally caused her to seek another church was a meeting she had with the minister — who was also the father of her best friend. To Stephanie he seemed more concerned about why she would not join than about why she should.

Stephanie and her mother found kindred spirits when they began attending Lehigh Valley Friends Meeting of Philadelphia Yearly Meeting and she began participating in the Young Friends group. She remembers especially feeling "for the first time that I really belonged somewhere." She was excited by the many youth retreats organized by a Philadelphia Yearly Meeting staff member with the assistance of First-day school teachers from meetings in east and southeast Pennsylvania, where the Young Friends usually went on weekend trips. One trip was to Quaker House in Washington, where they met with their congressmen, toured the Senate Building, and incidentally "saw who actually lived on Capitol Hill." Another memorable time was getting snowed in while visiting a host family in Kennett Square, and spending almost the entire weekend bird-watching, looking out their large kitchen window into their garden. And then the Young Friends had the experience of going to a depressed area in Philadelphia known as Mantua, where they painted two bedrooms in the home of an elderly woman and her incapacitated son. Stephanie's first uneasy feeling of finding herself in such a different environment was relieved by the warm reception from the black congregation where they attended church.

Many of the retreats were social and issue-oriented, where these teenage Young Friends were able to talk about feelings of alienation and the fears of growing up. It was a chance to share their thoughts about confusing issues during the period of the 1960s and early 1970s: war, nuclear holocaust, male-female relationships, and personal choices about such things as drugs and standards of social conduct. It was also here that she met a number of people who attended Quaker schools, and was encouraged to apply to one herself, even though it was a difficult decision for her family. After research and letter-writing, she made financial arrangements which included a generous scholarship from George School in Newtown, Pennsylvania, and enrolled there as a boarding student for her senior year in the fall of 1973. At George School she discovered attitudes of learning for learning's sake. Self-directed, independent lifelong learning became an important part of her philosophy. Later, when she herself was a teacher in the public schools of Monroe County, it became a goal she hoped to set for her students.

From George School, Stephanie went on to Earlham College, where she eventually met Bob Boenau. They were married under the care of Lehigh Valley Friends Meeting in 1979. While she appreciated the quality of the education that Earlham offered, she left after the fall semester of 1975 because she felt she was not ready to decide on a specific course of study. She went back home to Easton and worked as an assistant teacher in a federally subsidized day-care center for school-age children. It was there that she discovered her love for children, which planted the seed for her decision to become a teacher when she was able to resume her studies.

"But in order to do that," she said, "I needed to acquire Indiana residency by gaining a year's worth of work history. Before I knew it, one year had turned into three. I am very grateful, though, for the experiences I had working with people during that time." She worked in a nursing home south of Richmond while Bob was still at Earlham, and then for two years in Bloomington as a teacher's aide for slightly mentally handicapped children, and with the Title X remedial reading programs. She believes it was from these diverse groups of people, the elderly and the very young, that she learned patience and empathy. She said that remembering how humbled she was by the dignity she saw in the elderly residents in Richmond helped her later when faced with her own physical limitations.

After Stephanie received her bachelor's degree from Indiana University in 1982 with a K–12 endorsement for teaching mildly mentally handicapped, she substituted for a half-year and then was hired in early February 1983, first for a middle school learning disabilities class, and then the following year for a regular fourth-grade class at Lakeview elementary school in the southern part of Monroe County. There she taught third- to sixth-grade reading and English for six years, enjoying the relative freedom offered by a forward-looking public school, even though she was often frustrated by the lack of time for teaching and learning, by the difficulty of really getting to know her students, and by the lack of personal energy to do everything she thought needed to be done.

Two and a half years ago, a severe stroke obliged Stephanie to take a medical leave, and since then she has been learning about what is really important to her: relationships, love of life, personal religion, and music. She feels profoundly grateful for having this opportunity to take stock of her life, to make a fresh start, and to be thrilled by the little things in life. She gives much credit for her recovery to Bob's unflagging patience and encouragement. She loves having enough time and energy for cooking — collecting and creating vegetarian recipes with the goal of writing a cookbook. She enjoys gardening with Bob's help in preparing the soil with a rototiller. She had started with music in grade school, and over the years she has played clarinet, guitar, banjo, recorder, and piano, performing in music ensembles and in recorder groups. Now it is a joy to play and compose again with the help of a computer to take the place of her right hand.

For some time now, Stephanie has been coming with Bob to meeting for worship. "For too long," she says, "I have missed being among people who think about what they believe." She has joined a worship-sharing group, participated in spirituality discussions, shared "dinners for eight" in homes, and is currently clerk of the Library committee. She is a source of inspiration as she lives out her conviction that "religion is a search, and one's personal belief is not a place, but a path."

— Judy Edgerton, February 1993

QUAKER PROFILE No. 31:

Alice Elder Leake

Time spent with little children is always pure luxury for Alice. "One area where you are sure of what you are doing is loving a tiny child. Few people realize children grow by love, as well as by food," she says. "One can vicariously experience living in the present moment through interaction with the very young, who do this naturally." Our Friends First-day school had the rare good fortune of having Alice's leadership and presence for almost thirty years, beginning in 1961 when she and her husband Roy Leake and their two very young children came to Bloomington.

Now, after an absence, Alice is again among worshipers at meeting on First-days. She never left in spirit, while devoting full energies to the comfort and well-being of her family, especially her mother, Ruth Elder, who died last November after a long period of failing health. During much of that time, Alice found joy in the company of her first grandchild, Alyssa Stryker. Joy again entered the lives of the Leake family when Timothy was born to David and Caroline Leake here in Bloomington this past November.

Alice's special understanding of children and young people began with her own two older and three younger siblings in Iran (then Persia), where she was born and brought up, the daughter of Presbyterian missionaries, John and Ruth Roche Elder. She has memories from her early childhood in the town of Kermanshah, of abandoned babies so young that they were wet-nursed by her mother. In that culture of fanatic Mohammedanism, girls were often either killed or left at the door of Christian missionaries. Anyone who rejected Islam was punishable by death and forced into hiding. Missionary families did what they could in those tragic circumstances.

The Elder family lived in Hamadan from 1934 to 1937. There the children were home-schooled by their parents. They worked closely with the Armenian Christian church in a community of displaced persons. She underwent a religious crisis at the early age of seven when her best friend, a boy whose name was Billy Fisher, died of whooping cough. Unquestioning faith in God, so important in the circumstances of her everyday life, was shaken as she asked the question, "Why did Billy die? He never even got to visit America." In the minds of the children in this place where they witnessed ignorance and cruelty, going to America was second only to going to heaven. Later, she had a dream in which Billy came back and she was able to ask him the question. In the dream he answered, "I can't explain why I died. I only know I have to be here, and you there."

In 1937–38, before being stationed in the capital city, Teheran, the Elders traveled through prewar Europe. While they were in Germany, Alice's family worshiped in Pastor Martin Niemöller's Confessing Church, organized as part of an opposition to Adolf Hitler's efforts to bring the churches under his control. Back in Teheran in 1939, the family began to feel the full impact of the war raging over Europe. Refugees came from everywhere, including families with children fleeing from Germany, and Poles who had been crammed into boxcars for refuge in Africa, routed through Iran. There were twenty-eight nationalities in the international school the Elder children attended. It was hard to get basic supplies. American Army chaplains helped in getting food and water, and tried to keep the school staffed with teachers. Alice's Girl Scout troop made clothes from flour sacks for some of the orphans. Fighter planes from opposing armies scattered debris over the city. Alice was shocked when she saw guns belonging to British soldiers stacked outside the church and realized for the first time that not all Christians were pacifists.

Alice grew up in a family where pacifism was an unquestioned part of Christianity. As a young conscientious objector, Alice's father was on his way toward a lifetime devoted to removing the causes of war. He had worked with the Near East Foundation in Armenia when it was under siege by the Turks following World War I. He became isolated from other people working in his group while going in search of food for children left orphaned by a massacre. When he was reported to be dead, a 24-year-old Armenian Christian co-worker, Bodville Moodian, found him alive, risking his own life in the rescue. Later this man emigrated to Iran and was pastor of the Armenian Christian Church in Hamadan during the three years that the Elder family lived there.

In 1944, Americans were ordered out of the country. The Elders and two other missionary families refused to leave at that time. As a young teenager, Alice was sent to the United States ahead of her family, who followed a year later. On the voyage home in the company of a returning missionary and another child, she became aware of danger from floating mines. During the days that followed her arrival, she realized — with something like the shock experienced in adjusting to another culture — that America was not really next to heaven, as she and her deceased friend Billy Fisher had imagined at age seven. She was plunged into reality at Northfield School for Girls in Massachusetts, where she spent her last two years of secondary school. In the first place, she felt strange because she spoke with a British accent, owing to her associations in the international school in Teheran. Then she was appalled at the wastefulness of throwing so much away, including good food, that could be used by someone else. But most of all, she was mystified by the militaristic attitude even in the churches, emphasized by the final horror of the bombing of Nagasaki, Japan.

After high school, Alice went to Wellesley College, Massachusetts. With an eye toward nursing as a career, she worked in hospitals during summers. However, she decided on a teaching career, graduating from Wellesley in 1950 with a B.A. in history and sociology, and in 1951 from the Merrill Palmer School in Detroit with a certificate in preschool family development.

A Friends school would naturally welcome as a teacher someone with Alice's education as well as her belief in pacifism and social justice. She values the friendships she made during her two years of teaching at the Downingtown Friends School, mentioning in particular the William E. Cadbury family. A surprising part of her teaching experience was the biased attitude of a group of parents who wanted Alice fired because they found out she had voted for the Democrat Adlai Stevenson. One couple objected to black playmates for their little child in the school. Evidently, parents whose children attend Friends schools for the educational benefits are not necessarily acquainted with Quaker principles! In 1953–54, Alice faced new challenges working with seriously disturbed children in the laboratory nursery school at Eastern Psychiatric Hospital. When she learned that, after treatment, some of the children were sent back to homes with parents who were themselves psychotic, she felt uncertain about the system and frustrated by her inability to make a lasting difference in the lives of these children.

Her next year of teaching was at Haverford Friends School. That year 1954–55 was a fateful one for Alice, for some Friends she knew well were also well acquainted with Roy Leake. These Friends decided that the two young idealists should be introduced. It was an instant and lasting attraction, and they were married under the care of Radnor Friends Meeting on August 7, 1954. True to his pacifist convictions, Roy was a conscientious objector who had been in Civilian Public Service Camp and had done Quaker relief work in France and in the French zone of occupied Germany following World War II. When they met, Roy had returned to the United States and was in charge of the Philadelphia office of a life insurance company. The couple started life together in a two-room apartment over the garage on the premises of Reed and Margaret Cary in Germantown, now a part of Philadelphia. Their two children, Patricia and David, were born while they lived there. Meanwhile, Roy took a position in the financial office of the American Friends Service Committee in Philadelphia. Deciding on an academic career, he then began work toward his Ph.D. in French at Bryn Mawr College.

After completing his course work in 1961, he joined the Department of French and Italian at Indiana University; and the family moved to Bloomington, becoming active members of our Friends meeting. Alice said that when they first bought the house where they now live in Bloomington, it was in run-down condition, and Friends from the meeting formed a work party and painted it for them.

Roy and Alice and the children spent the academic year 1967–68 in Strasbourg, France, where Roy was director of the Indiana-Purdue foreign study program for forty university students. From 1970 to 1974, they spent eight weeks each summer at St.-Brieuc, France, in charge of the honors program in French for Indiana high school students. This was an important period in the life of the Leake family, for Patsy and David, then in their early teens, experienced a foreign culture in depth and became fluent in French, as did Alice herself.

It is not easy to recount the vital part Alice and Roy have played in the life of our meeting over the past thirty-two years. We have mentioned the twenty-eight years during which Alice used her skills working with the youngest children in First-day school. Both she and Roy have served as recording clerk for the meeting, have attended regional meetings, and have done prison visitation. Roy is presently working in the rehabilitation of young offenders. They started the meeting's active outreach to young Friends at the university, seeking them out from the lists of students' religious preferences that the university provided at that time, and then inviting the students to their home on Sunday evenings. They saw the need for a Meeting newsletter and began publishing it with the use of a mimeograph machine while meetings for worship were still being held in the Seventh Day Adventist Church building, before we acquired a meetinghouse of our own.

Many books and personalities have played a part in Alice's religious journey. Her mother, also a graduate of Wellesley College and a major influence in Alice's life, had given up her own career to join her husband as a missionary. Her father, a scholar as well as a missionary, translated numerous books into Persian and wrote a history of the Reformation in that language. It was a meaningful experience for Alice to read the writings of the sixteenth-century philosopher and essayist Michel de Montaigne, assisting Roy in the preparation of material for his book on the subject. She mentioned *The Practice of the Presence of God* by the seventeenth century Carmelite friar Brother Lawrence; the famous chapter on the legend of the Grand Inquisitor in Dostoyevsky's novel *The Brothers Karamazov*; and the twentieth-century play *J.B.*, by Archibald MacLeish. In her early acquaintance with Quakerism, Alice found some of the Pendle Hill pamphlets to be especially helpful. Not least in her list is Anna Pettit Brommell's *A Quaker Story Caravan*, a collection of stories for children, which she read in First-day school. Her mother enjoyed hearing them read aloud in the waning days of her life.

Alice also values the close ties she had with individual Quakers during the decade spent in the Philadelphia area. She has a sense of gratitude and admiration for those whose faith and action founded Bloomington Friends Meeting. She sees the same spirit in the Meeting today as it deals with complicated issues by focusing on the facts, concerns, and ramifications involved before taking positive action.

In a Catholic orphanage in Detroit as part of her graduate training, Alice was given the care of a tiny neglected baby who was dying because it would not eat. She was assigned to hold the baby continuously for one whole weekend. Feeling the human touch, the baby responded and lived. "A child who is loved responds and grows," she said. Speaking of the nearly three decades of work with young children in our First-day school, she says she was rewarded "because showing love to little ones goes beyond merely teaching into the realm of understanding that knows no language."

— Judy Edgerton, March 1993

QUAKER PROFILE No. 32:

Judith Ellen Davis

Judy Davis's religious philosophy is the foundation for the professional care she gives on a daily basis to suffering people. She says of her work, "It is a unique job where spirituality is an important ingredient." She is a psychiatric nurse working with the Indianapolis branch of the Visiting Nurse Service, a national organization founded by nurses in the early part of this century. She summarized the overwhelming ramifications of her work by saying that she makes it possible for psychiatric patients to live in their own homes rather than in institutions.

Judy calls on all her resources to meet the challenge. In the first place, she must have a comfortable personal relationship with people whose views of the world are distorted. With basic trust established, she can then take care of their medical needs. And finally, she must make decisions about their living conditions and see that the necessary steps are taken to implement them.

She emphasized the challenge to be tolerant and nonjudgmental, to really listen to her patients. She says that she basically likes people, and enjoys getting to know them. She is grateful for her own firmly established religious foundation, which gives her the self-confidence to listen dispassionately to the sometimes extreme, even bizarre religious preoccupations of many of her patients.

Impromptu counseling is a large part of each encounter with a patient in his or her home. Grasping the total situation,

Judy must find out whether the patient is taking prescribed medication or, in the case of some patients, whether they neglect, forget, or refuse medication altogether. She decides whether there should be a change in medication or dosage, and whether a counselor is needed. For patients whose blood must be tested, she draws the blood for the laboratory. In certain types of medication, such as for insulin-dependent diabetics, she fills the syringes with a week's supply.

Once their medical needs are met, she must not only advise the patients about their continued medication but also check on practical matters of day-to-day living: Does the patient have adequate help? Does he or she need someone to stay with them — a companion or a "sitter"? How often should the home nurse or nurse's aide come in? What is the patients' economic situation? Do they have the benefit of Medicare/Medicaid? How cost-effective is the kind of treatment they are receiving?

Judy's little Subaru takes her approximately three hundred miles a week on her rounds through six counties and home again to her cottage on Lake LaSalle in the hills of Brown County. There she is renewed by the sounds and sights of birds and trees and water. She learned to love that natural environment from her widowed grandmother Davis, who had a cabin in Brown County where Judy often spent time as a child. The grandmother taught her the skills and delights of camping, hiking, and fishing. She was a bird-watcher, and Judy acquired from her an appreciation for wildlife and living with nature.

The Davis family home was in Southport, Indiana, a small town just south of Indianapolis and north of Greenwood. Judy grew up with an older brother, Timothy, and parents Joseph and Dolores Davis. Church was not a part of her early childhood, but it abruptly became a focal point of family participation when she was twelve years old and her father was persuaded by a Pentacostal co-worker to become a Christian. In the language of that sect, the co-worker "witnessed" to Judy's father, so that he "accepted Jesus as his personal Savior." The family decided to join the United Presbyterian church. Time spent during her teen years in the company of other Presbyterian young people is a positive memory for

Judy. The emphasis was on outreach and helping other people, with the feeling of being one big extended family. Church members worked as families, helping with adult literacy and going into inner-city Indianapolis to repair homes for the poor. However, Judy recalls that as a questioning teenager, she was dismissed with "Don't question the teachings of the church; just have faith." She does not consider herself a student of the Bible, although she has read it through twice.

Judy described her mother as liking the company of other people, comfortably exchanging time previously spent with bridge-playing friends for the close associations she formed while working with the church. Just as Judy was entering the University of Evansville at age eighteen, her father died. She describes him as a fun-loving man and a good musician, who used his talents to entertain. She inherited his gift, enjoys singing, and plays popular, contemporary piano music.

Since obtaining her bachelor of science degree in nursing in 1975, Judy has steadily grown in her sympathetic understanding of people who suffer from mental illness or emotional distress. Two internships before graduation gave her early firsthand experience. The first was in England during the first half of her senior year, when she worked with the National Health Service. There she was confirmed in the belief that "health is a right, not a privilege," rather than the other way around as it is in our own country. The second apprenticeship was in the mountains of southeastern Kentucky. There she learned to appreciate differing personalities and approaches in life, as she traveled by Jeep ministering to the needs of people scattered through isolated places among the hills and hollows.

Following graduation, Judy worked for seven years with psychologically damaged veterans at Veterans Army Hospital in Indianapolis. There she witnessed firsthand the effects of war on the lives of those who go into battle. These veterans were from three wars: World War II, the Korean War, and the Vietnam War. In addition to the trauma of war itself, the use of drugs created psychiatric problems and permanent brain damage. Judy learned to know some of her patients well and heard many war stories. We are not surprised that she has explored two peace churches, the Mennonites and the Brethren, and now has become a member of a third, the Quakers. She also experienced the reassuring teachings of Unity church for a period of time, but she came to prefer her own Inner Light, or Christ Within, rather than leaning on an intermediary in the person of a pastor.

Judy made a professional change of pace following her years at the V.A. hospital. First she taught the sciences, including biology, in a public high school in Indianapolis. Then she continued to work with students as part of her duties with the Public Health department in that city. She taught basic health to older students, and did sight and hearing testing and immunization for younger children, along with helping to recognize cases of child abuse. After this interlude, she returned to nursing and worked with employers and patients from industry in workers' compensation insurance. As we have said, she now enjoys making it possible for her patients to live in their own homes.

Long hours, together with the necessity of making fateful decisions affecting other people, are a way of life for the health-care professional. Nevertheless, Judy has found time not only for taking courses leading to a master's degree in her field of psychiatric nursing, but also for personal development. She mentioned reading Ernest Holmes's *Science of Mind*, and also a collection of essays and articles from journals, entitled *A Course in Miracles*, published by the Foundation for Inner Peace. She was profoundly moved by the woman who called herself Peace Pilgrim. This person, who finally died in a car accident, had walked across the United States several times, speaking about a way to inner peace and vowing to walk until peace was universal. Judy's Quaker reading has included the writings of Leonard Kenworthy and Rufus Jones, and also Jessamyn West's *Quaker Reader*.

Following a period when she did not attend church, Judy explored Catholicism, Episcopalianism, and Judaism, in addition to the peace churches mentioned earlier. She was attracted to the idea of meditation, and looked up Quakers in the telephone directory, coming to her first meeting for worship on a Sunday morning in November of 1991. Her experience was like a sigh upon resting after a long journey; for she said, as others in our Meeting have also said, "At that first service, it was like coming home." We welcome home this new member, with her innate love of people and her own life dedicated to making the lives of people in distress more tolerable.

— Judy Edgerton, April 1993

QUAKER PROFILE No. 33:

Barbara Anne Bolz

"Sometimes I sit in meeting for worship and feel gratitude for how constant God is."

Barbara said this as her words about her religious journey flowed in a clear, exuberant stream. She spoke of her recent decision to become a member of the Society of Friends as a part of having gradually grown in understanding of her own spirituality. She said that her upbringing in a Church of Christ laid the foundation upon which she has built her mature religious life. During her late teens and early twenties she became indifferent to organized religion, but she never doubted the existence of God as an ever-present force.

Continuous study of the Bible, in the church and in the family, is the central focus in the Churches of Christ, as Barbara described them. These churches developed from various religious movements in the United States in the early part of the last century. They believe in the all-sufficiency of the Bible without need of a creed; and each church is an autonomous unit. Baptism by immersion was recorded in the New Testament; therefore, immersion is deemed to be necessary in order to be a Christian. Because there is no reference to musical instruments in the earliest churches according to the biblical record, Churches of Christ sing their hymns without accompaniment. They try to follow in a direct line from the first-century churches, and tend to be exclusive with regard to people outside their faith. There was Bible study in the church on Sunday morning, Sunday night, and Wednesday night, and study at home with the family on Tuesday night. Barbara memorized Bible verses and participated in contests about scriptural knowledge.

Barbara loved those hymns sung a cappella in her church. On a recent Sunday evening when the regular hymn singing before Friends meeting for worship had been precluded by an early-morning discussion group, she went to the evening service at a very small Church of Christ in order to satisfy her need for expression in song. As a young person in that closed society, she had become aware that many of the hymns they were singing had been written by people who were not in Churches of Christ at all, and so in the words of the hymns she had begun to feel the impact of religious experiences expressed by Christians belonging to different sects. Today she has the same appreciation for experiencing other people's perceptions through the messages of Friends who speak out of the silence in meetings for worship.

While participating in that recent Church of Christ evening service, Barbara became aware that she was now an outsider among the worshipers there. But she realized too, from her Quaker perspective, that this exclusion called forth no resentment within her, but only the insight that all groups worship God according to their own lights. Through friendship with a colleague who is a devout fundamentalist, she has learned that religious conservatives can still be compassionate. She said that a verse by Edwin Markham's poem "Outwitted," quoted by a worshiper in Friends Meeting, expressed how she now feels about exclusiveness:

> He drew a circle that shut me out —
> Heretic, rebel, a thing to flout.
> But love and I had the wit to win:
> We drew a circle that took him in.

Although the questioning she went through as she was reaching adulthood caused her to leave the Church of Christ, her habit from childhood of constantly thinking about God remained strong. She continued to feel a reassuring presence that found expression as a sensation she described as something like the ringing of a bell when she took a forward step in her spiritual journey. She talks of this experience as a strong leading in relationship with God. She says she had the sensation of a ringing bell when a Friends Meeting member asked her, "When are you going to become a member?" She describes the interim years after leaving her childhood church and before her searching brought her to mature, reasoned decisions, as a time when the life of the spirit was in a state of flux. "Through all my wandering and searching, God has stayed with me," she said. "I think of a very special Sunday school teacher I had at the time I was in fifth grade. She loved us kids, and when she went to Australia as a missionary, she sent me a coin and a card that read: 'Remember, God loves you.' That has stayed with me."

The concept of family is important to Barbara, first her own birth family, and now the new family unit she has established with Kath Pennavaria. Barbara was born in Germany, where her father was stationed as a U.S. Air Force career officer. While Barbara was growing up, the family moved to a number of locations in the States, living all the while in military housing. This gave her the feeling that she lacked ties and roots. Her family consisted of her parents, Richard Edward Bolz and Peggy Marie Newsom Bolz; a brother, Gary; and a sister, Lise Marie, who later changed her name to Nadezhka. Gary has stayed with his fundamentalist religious upbringing and is now a missionary for the Church of Christ in Italy. Nadezhka is a six-foot-one-inch stand-up comic, who sometimes shaves her head, and expresses her spirituality outside organized religion. Since retiring from the Air Force, Barbara's father holds seminars in computer language, known as Ada, for the Department of Defense. His seminar work has decreased with the end of the Cold War, but he once told Barbara that he would still have voted for peace if it had ever been on a referendum. Her mother went to college after the children were grown, obtained a master's degree in social work from the University of Denver in Colorado, and now has a private practice in therapy.

"Family defines who you are," Barbara says. She feels deeply about the commitment she and Kath have to each other, and says they hope to settle in one place and establish the roots she missed as a child. The inner bell rang when she became acquainted with Kath, giving her the feeling that she was centered and was on the right path. After five years, on

July 4, 1992, a few friends gathered in an outdoor setting to read poetry and sing songs, marking the lifelong commitment of Barbara and Kath to each other. Kath is working toward certification to teach English in high school. They are adding a child to their family when Kath gives birth in the fall to a baby conceived by artificial insemination. They lead a peaceful life, praying together each night, seeking God in connectedness with the life force that Barbara feels as she focuses her petition on the growing fetus. Elise Boulding's Pendle Hill pamphlet, *Born Remembering*, holds special meaning for her, as it deals with our innate linkage with the Divine — an hourly, daily Presence that haunts each new life from its very beginning.

Barbara's B.A. in English literature is from the University of Colorado and her M.A. from the University of Missouri. She has now completed her course work for a Ph.D. in English at Indiana University. She teaches undergraduates at the university, writes on assignment for our local newspaper, the *Herald-Times*, and regularly takes classified ads by telephone at the newspaper each Friday and on alternate Saturdays. She is preparing for the Ph.D. qualifying examination at the end of this summer, 1993. She is well along with research for her dissertation, which is to deal with autobiographies of American Quaker women. The focus is to be on what God means in the lives of these women. She says there is nothing more precious for her than reading the thoughts and experiences that these women chronicled as valued parts of their everyday —and often extraordinary — lives.

The pressures of Barbara's work are relieved when she sculls on Lake Lemon and hikes on the path around Griffy Lake, feeling the presence of God as she sings and prays. She recognizes birds by sight and by their song, both on these outings and at her home. With weekday schedules so full, she still sets aside time on Sunday mornings for hymn singing and silent worship with Friends, for volunteering to help with the children and teens when needed and to serve food and drinks after worship and at shared meals. She will assume new committee responsibilities when the Meeting year changes in midsummer. In silent worship, she is often haunted early on with a message, then asks God whether she should stand up and speak. She does so only if she cannot remain seated, feeling something like an invisible force pushing her out of her seat. She feels inarticulate and afraid her message is not clear, but afterwards has a sense of relief that the struggle against speaking is over.

A part of becoming an adult has been examining her childhood and deciding which values are to be retained at this stage in her spiritual journey. Meanwhile, she says of Friends Meeting, "This is my spiritual home."

— Judy Edgerton, May 1993

QUAKER PROFILE No. 34:

Mary Patricia Goodman Anderson

One should not be deceived by Mary Anderson's quiet manner. Underneath is a strength and a resolve that fuel the energies for her accomplishments. "I am a firm believer in dreams combined with effort," she said. "I love the four-line verse written in my high school yearbook by my art teacher: 'One seed can start a garden, / One drop can start a sea, / One doubt can start a hating, / One dream can set us free.' "

Devoting herself to the work required of a dedicated member of the Religious Society of Friends seems to come naturally for Mary. It is part of her ability to prioritize her time so as to concentrate on the task at hand. For the past three years, she has been teaching architecture, computer drafting, and related courses at Indiana Vocational Technical College. She also does freelance design and drafting and has designed a number of local residential additions. She often says she wishes for more time to devote to her family; but it is evident that her three children are sharing her goals, learning self-reliance, and seeing her as a role model for professional success within a religious life.

Bloomington Friends Meeting has been indebted during the past year to Mary's leadership as clerk of Ministry and Counsel, the committee that is most responsible for the spiritual life of our meeting. In addition to both routine responsibilities and unpredictable problems as head of Ministry and Counsel, she found time to help organize our part in the

Chain of Prayer for Friends United Meeting and the spring retreat held at the meetinghouse. Immediately upon arriving in Bloomington in July 1989, she began working with the Religious Education Committee and as a teacher in First-day school. Public recognition of her leadership came with her approval by the Monthly Meeting to be a member of Ministry and Counsel in July 1991, only eight months after she became a member of the meeting.

Mary attributes the foundation for her life of the spirit to experience in her early years. She was raised in a strongly Catholic family and attended Catholic schools through the eighth grade. She is deeply appreciative of her religious heritage. There is a pervading sense of mystery that she associates with the Catholic Church. She was moved by the litany, music, and pageantry of pre-Easter Lent and Easter; she found joy in anticipation as preparations were made for Christmas; and she loved the beautiful use of flowers in the Crowning of Mary ceremony in the month of May. "I had a place in it," she said. "I belonged."

Mary's talents as a leader were put to a test in her early teens when she taught religious studies in Saturday school. She was involved in outreach as a member of her youth group, remembering especially the contacts she had with residents in a nursing home when she read to them.

Mary was born in Scottsbluff, Nebraska. Her family moved to Longmont, Colorado, when she was thirteen. She speaks warmly of her parents, Vern Goodman and Patricia McBride Goodman. Her middle name, Patricia, is for her mother, and she was called Patti at home. She is the middle child, with an older sister and brother and two younger brothers. She named them for us in order of birth: Cynthia, Mike, then Mary, Mathias, and Tony. The youngest was adopted just as Mary was entering her teen years. She felt proud and responsible as a big sister to her baby brother, she said. "The hands-on experience I got made me comfortable with mothering. And I saw the joy my parents had in their adopted son."

And so adoption seemed natural in later years when Mary had established her own family. She met Jonathan Anderson when he was a practice teacher and she was a senior in high school. They were married in the summer of 1975 in Fort Collins, Colorado, when she was eighteen. Daughters Emily and Alicia (Tia) were born in Washington, D.C., and son Justin was adopted as an infant when Mary and Jonathan were in Bangladesh in 1980.

In addition to the example in her own Goodman family, the happy blend of adopted and birth children belonging to Jonathan's sister and brother-in-law was a factor in their decision to adopt a baby. Mary says that she and Jonathan satisfied their wish to have another child without adding to the overpopulation of the planet. And also, "we simply wanted a baby boy to raise and watch grow up with our daughters."

The new baby, less than one week old, came from an orphanage in Bangladesh where Mary did volunteer work while Jonathan served there as a State Department Foreign Service officer. During three years before that assignment, their home had been in Washington, D.C., where Jonathan obtained a master's degree in public administration from American University. Emily was born in a hospital, and Tia was born at home with the assistance of a midwife. Mary was busy at that time not only with a toddler and an infant; she also managed the home of a 95-year-old retired Presbyterian minister and drove him to his various appointments. She said the interaction between the elderly man, whom she called Doc, and little Emily was wonderful. Those days were crowded with joys, struggles, and meaningful experiences for the young mother. A course in liturgical dance that she took at Georgetown University "combined my love of spiritual music with movement," and she enjoyed sharing it with her parents at their twenty-fifth wedding anniversary. She and Jonathan made good friends in the Church of the Brethren they attended in Kensington, Maryland, just outside Washington. She found one particular ritual followed by that church to be very moving. The rituals of the Church of the Brethren include a foot-washing ceremony as a sign of humility, following the account in the New Testament when Jesus washed his disciples' feet at the Last Supper (John 13:3-17).

Mary refers to the time she spent in Washington and during Jonathan's Foreign Service experience in Bangladesh and Australia as her "growing years," which served to heighten her sense of religious and social responsibility. Describing it as "an evolution of things believed in," she specifically mentioned peace and the sanctity of life, saying that she does not condone either abortion or capital punishment. She disagrees with members of religious groups who insist that the fetus be protected and yet advocate capital punishment. "I am strongly Christian," she says, "but I have difficulty believing that the Bible is the only word of God. After living in other parts of the world, I believe there are many paths to God. The spirit in Friends Meeting seems to reflect that belief. I had never joined a church since leaving the Catholic faith. In many ways, becoming a Quaker has felt like putting the parts of myself together. I also have a sense of being able to be who I am and being accepted for myself and my own path to God — something I haven't felt before."

Mary and Jonathan had briefly attended a programmed Friends church in Fort Collins before their marriage, but their first close contact with Quakerism occurred when they returned to Washington after their two years in Bangladesh and a one-year assignment in Australia. During the following year, they attended an unprogrammed preparative meeting in Herndon, Virginia, just outside Washington, that was under the care of Langley Hill Friends Meeting. It was six years after that when they moved to Bloomington and our Friends meeting. During those six years, the family lived in Bozeman, Montana, where Mary became a full-time student in a five-year program leading to a degree in architecture at Montana State University. At the same time, she looked after her family and helped with a taxi business that she and Jonathan owned. "During that time," she said, "I came to appreciate more and more the friendship, love, strength, and support of Jonathan and the security and joy of family ties. I could not have made it without them."

She said that when the time came to choose a topic for her architecture thesis, there was no doubt about what it should be. A concern for the situation of orphaned children, combined with her study of architecture, led to a project that took her back to Bangladesh, and to India, to do research for the thesis. In those two countries she saw in action a program for the upbringing of orphans in small homes rather than in large institutions. The individual homes are clustered in groups, or villages, called S.O.S. (Save Our Souls). To care for the many orphaned children following World War II, the Austrians pioneered under the leadership of Hermann Gmiener in setting up homes for eight to ten children under the care of a widow or other single woman who became their mother for life. Each village has a library, a day-care facility, and a health clinic. Kinderdorf International (Children's Village International) is the organizing body. There are now more than 250 S.O.S. orphan villages worldwide. For her thesis leading to the degree of bachelor of architecture, Mary designed a village suitable for use in Calcutta, India.

While Mary has used her skills and training here in Bloomington as described in the opening paragraphs of this profile, Jonathan has been working toward a doctorate in the School of Public and Environmental Affairs at Indiana University. Emily is a junior in high school, Tia is in the ninth grade, and Justin is in the sixth grade. This fall, Mary plans to go to the University of Illinois at Champaign-Urbana, 150 miles away, where she will be working on her master of architecture degree with a specialty in facilities management. She will be back in Bloomington with her family on weekends, and she says, "I'm sure that in the coming year I will be needing the meeting for worship as a time and place of renewal, and I'm thankful to know that it will be there for me."

"One seed can start a garden . . ."

— Judy Edgerton, July 1993

QUAKER PROFILE: No. 35:

John Wright Daschke

John Daschke's approach to Quakerism and religion is that of a scholar, but underneath is his own deep reverence from early childhood for the Eternal Christ. The child developed into a teenaged seeker of truth. His first encounter with Quakers came at a religious retreat for students from a number of private schools when he was fifteen years old. He was drawn to the door of a conference room in a hotel where the retreat was being held, then went in when the door was opened for latecomers, and found he was in a Friends meeting. The ordinary struggles and pains of adolescence had been multiplied by traumatizing circumstances for John; but he says, "I went in, sat down, and felt at peace."

John had been taken to the religious retreat by the chaplain of a private school in rural Pennsylvania, where he lived year-round from age eleven until he graduated in 1965. He was virtually without family, because his father had died of a heart attack when John was seven years old, and his mother was chronically ill and hospitalized much of the time. On the advice of a social worker, his care and upbringing was entrusted entirely to the school. He was separated from his two sisters, who were each placed in a different foster home. He was a superior student and a leader, managing by sheer will to survive in a prison-like atmosphere where the twelve hundred young boys at the school were ruled by harsh physical discipline. John was antithetical to violence then, as he is today. On one occasion, he intervened on behalf of a child who was in mortal danger, lying in a fetal position while a housemother was kicking him.

Trapped by rules and demands of strict conformity, the sensitive teenager was not at peace with being forced to compromise on what he felt was wrong at that school. Arbitrary discipline by individual teachers and staff kept the boys in a state of watchful anxiety. Heavily endowed by a manufacturing philanthropist, the vocational school had been set up early in this century on a very large tract of land. In order to be admitted, a boy had to be physically and mentally fit, and orphaned by at least one of his parents. It was entirely free, but there were many chores, often long working hours, and no frills. One illustration was the requirement for a growing child to wear one pair of shoes for three years, the third year for rough farm work. The governing board seemed to be obsessed with operating as cheaply as possible, while maintaining the best possible public image. The philosophy of early boys' schools both here and abroad was that a harsh, cold environment was in the best interests of the students. Sometimes sympathetic staff members were able to "bend the rules" and soften the discipline. John survived, and excelled academically. He was one of six boys chosen for achievement, verbal skills, and personality to show off the school on such occasions as at civic club meetings and the religious retreat mentioned above where he first encountered Quakerism.

John Wright Daschke was born in Ridley Park, Pennsylvania, near Philadelphia. He has an older sister, Marjorie, and a younger sister, Mary. Their parents were Marjorie Jean and August John Daschke. The family moved first to suburban Chatham Park and then, after his father's early death, to Manoa.

John was born with a metabolic defect that made him unable to tolerate lactose in milk. His parents followed their doctor's instructions and fed him a soy-based substitute, but his maternal grandmother intervened and persuaded them that she could "cure" him by a combination of harsh home remedies and a dose of self-discipline. The result was a near tragedy when he became so ill that, according to his mother, he was clinically dead. He believes this near-death experience may have given him a heightened insight upon which he has always based his reactions to groups with varying religious philosophies. He says he remained "cold and unmoved by the right-wing fundamentalist mandatory Sunday services" at the school where he grew up. As a young child, while living with relatives or in foster homes, he had gone to a Church of Christ kindergarten and Sunday school, and to several different kinds of church services. For as long as he can remember, he has known Christ. "My view of the Eternal Christ," he says, "is as man's connection to the incomprehensible, eternal, ineffable, universal God. My physical image of the Eternal Christ is a brilliant Light, containing all visible colors and others not visible. That Light has grown from the maximum conceivable size and brilliance for the toddler who first saw it, to the maximum conceivable size and brilliance for the person I am now. That Light grows and brightens in the presence of Friends and other devout persons, and my personal view of that Light gains some from each such sharing of Light."

John told us that he has grown from all his past experiences. His pain at being neglected and abused by those who should have loved him most has resulted in "empathy with anyone who is excluded or stereotyped rather than treated as a unique child of God." Those who sustained him as a boy during times when he was in need of help often belonged to denigrated minorities. "Every good and decent act I observe," he said, "persuades me that God's grace is not exclusive to a chosen few, but available to all who accept it without regard to the label they carry."

When we in Bloomington Friends Meeting speak of John, we are apt to say "John and Lary." The couple first met in Eigenmann Hall on the campus of Indiana University when they were both graduate students. They were married in August of 1973. Lary Smith is a published writer of both poetry and fiction, written in medieval settings. She uses the pen name Frida Westford. She holds advanced degrees in French, comparative literature, and library science.

John's academic field is political science. He was granted the Ph.D. degree from Indiana University in 1985. He had been one of two at the top of his graduating class from his secondary school, and then entered the Massachusetts Institute of Technology at the age of sixteen. He decided to change his course of study, transferred to the American University in Washington, D.C., and graduated summa cum laude in 1970, coming to Indiana University in the fall of that year. The sudden death of the Indiana University professor whom he refers to as his mentor, Václav Beneš, was a personal tragedy, and also resulted in major dislocation in the proceedings necessary for John's doctoral degree. He was fortunate to be selected in 1973 by IREX (the International Research and Exchanges Board) to spend a year in Czechoslovakia for research on his dissertation. The absence of normal support by an advisor during the completion of his dissertation and the general shift of interest from his specialized area in political science have been a hindrance to the advancement of his career in teaching. Nevertheless, he has had two successful short-term teaching assignments in higher education, has had a responsible role in an Indiana environmental organization, and has done short-term teaching in the Monroe County public school system. One might observe that roadblocks in the way of advancement in his chosen field have given him time for concentrated Quaker work. John himself concurs in this and says, "I have substituted work with the Friends Committee on National Legislation, the Peace and Social Concerns Committee of Bloomington Friends Meeting, and the Committee on Christian Social Concerns of Western Yearly Meeting for the professional opportunities that I lost." He says he is interested in politics as a way to social justice, and finds working with the FCNL to be particularly rewarding.

And that is by no means the total of John's varied interests. Technological skills come naturally, so he has enjoyed working as a computer operator, technician, and consultant. His hobbies are scale-modeling sailing ships, and nature photography. Nowadays, though, the family cat with the Czech name of Kočka finds John's little animal subjects for his photography too tempting as playful, pouncing targets! Even his choice of political science as a discipline for study may possibly have resulted from the early necessity to figure out the cause and effect of events in his daily existence. Today he enjoys observing as people interact around him, then figuring out for himself, as he said, "what makes them tick."

We began John's profile by saying that a mature attitude and a scholarly approach to religion have been added to his early childhood attraction to the Eternal Christ. He has been influenced by wide reading in the social and physical sciences and also in religious studies, where he is as inclined to use books on history or archaeology as books of religious commentary. He has read and reread the Quaker classics, the *Journal of George Fox*, the *Journal of John Woolman*, and Robert Barclay's *Apology*. He also reads current materials, such as Leonard Kenworthy's *Quakerism: A Study Guide*, the Pendle Hill pamphlets, and the Quaker journals. As a young child who had only just learned to read well, he tried vainly to comprehend the Bible. He says that he had to "wait for mature judgment to find out that the Bible was a stream-of-consciousness discovery of God, running from 3200 B.C. to about 100 A.D. Ideas originating in an early era and written down about 600 B.C. depicted the Hebrew God as a vengeful patriarch, a tribal god confined to his temple, and only one of many gods. I never could understand people who claimed that these ideas were just as valid as the words of Jesus. I see the Bible as a testimony to spiritual growth, which has continued to this day. The idea of continuing revelation seems self-evident." John's reading of books on Middle Eastern archeology and on biblical history, along with his professional training, have caused him to see that "the priestly writers of Leviticus in the Old Testament were concerned with maintaining and enhancing their own power and making the Hebrews distinct and separate, whereas the Christian message derived from Jesus' teachings is inclusive."

John sampled a number of Quaker meetings after that first one when he was a boy of fifteen. Before coming to Bloomington in 1970, he had gone to Meetings in the Washington, D.C., area and had attended Haverford Friends Meeting in Pennsylvania. In 1974, he and Lary attended Bloomington Friends Meeting for the first time with some regularity. His initial attraction was to the Peace and Social Concerns committee, in which he has played an active role. He has also worked with the Friends on Campus committee, with a view to meeting the needs and interests of students interested in Quakerism. He has been our Meeting's contact with the Friends Committee on National Legislation since 1987 and Western Yearly Meeting's representative to the General Committee of FCNL since 1988, and he attends the annual meetings.

John expresses himself as always being repelled by self-righteous religious authority. He says that his most moving spiritual experiences during his adult life have been in gathered meetings for worship in a meetinghouse, or in those held as a part of the FCNL annual meetings. "I am increasingly open to the guiding visions that come to me in those circumstances," he says. Quakerism is the way his mind and spirit work, helping him to find his way through adversity and then to grow from that adversity. It leads him to new insights, and lessens his chronic tendencies to anxiety and depression. He is grateful that it has given him confidence to be uncompromising in some choices in his professional life, leaving him at peace with himself, in contrast to his teen years when he was often forced to comply in order to survive in that dictatorial environment.

In his letter of application for membership in January of this year, John said: "I have been a convinced Friend for over twenty years, and committed to Bloomington Friends Meeting for the past fifteen years. . . . I invented most of the basic Friends beliefs for myself before discovering Friends. . . . As a Christ-centered universalist, I confuse everybody, including myself, but I am comfortable with any individual path to the Eternal Christ as long as they don't try to impose that path as the only one."

John is indeed in the tradition of the Quaker seeker after truth. His personal revelations are continually being tested by questioning, listening, and study. Bloomington Monthly Meeting and Western Yearly Meeting are the fortunate beneficiaries of his insights, and of the planning and execution of tasks undertaken by him on behalf of us all.

—Judy Edgerton, August 1993

QUAKER PROFILE No. 36:

Terrill Layton Cosgray

With Terrill Cosgray's knowledge of the Scriptures and his personal relationship with a mystical Presence such as Thomas Kelly wrote about, he is solidly placed in the mystical Quaker tradition from its beginnings to the present. He has reread Kelly's *Testament of Devotion* several times, and clearly identifies with him. Terry says that after extensive reading and searching, he was attracted to the experiential approach to religion that is a part of Quakerism. George Fox, the founder of Quakerism in the seventeenth century, said of his religious "openings": "And this I know experimentally." William Penn commented on Fox's extraordinary gift in explaining the Scriptures.

On two occasions in times of deep despair, Terry has had a sense of God's physical presence which has marked changes on two levels in the direction of his life. A sentence from Thomas Kelly is particularly apt: "Between the two levels is fruitful interplay, but ever the accent must be upon the deeper level, where the soul ever dwells in the presence of the Holy One."

The first of these two experiences of the presence of God took place on March 7, 1977, the day the Cosgrays' daughter, Camellia, was born here in Bloomington. Terry and his English wife, Elizabeth Gwynn Cosgray (Libby), had left California with their eight-month-old son Nathan in the summer of 1976, after Terry's graduation from the University of California at Santa Barbara. According to Libby, "All our possessions were in our car, and it wasn't a very big car"; and according to Terry, their assets totaled only six hundred dollars. By the end of the year they had settled in Bloomington, drawn here in part by their desire to live in a university town, in part by an article in the *National Geographic* about southern Indiana, and in part by Terry's own memories of his first eleven years of life in his Hoosier birthplace, Logansport. On that momentous spring day, the joy of welcoming a second baby brought with it a realization that the circumstances surrounding his life were out of his control.

Government-subsidized housing and Terry's job in a fast-food restaurant had kept the family on a subsistence level when they first arrived in Bloomington. Terry, a vegetarian, worked under stressful conditions, one of which was his repulsion to the point of illness that he experienced when having to handle meat. Finally, on that March day, he found it impossible to continue in the job. In despair over his inability to provide for his helpless young family, he threw himself on his bed and wept. "There in my agony," he recalled, "I had a sense of God's physical presence. I knew a way was opening. It was an undergirding experience, one that left me feeling calmly assured that God was in charge." A job he had applied for at the Bloomington Hospital came through three days after his vivid realization of the presence of God. Terry continued, "In similar experiences of despair since then, God has always been there. I know one can't abuse God's care by taking wrong actions, ones taken without careful thought. But if you are doing your best to follow a leading, then a way will open. You may have to go through despair and trauma again — it has happened before and will happen again. This has been my experience."

A second severe crisis overwhelmed Terry nine years later, in 1986, when he and Libby experienced serious marital problems. On the verge of a divorce and unable to live together, they crossed the Atlantic separately. While she visited her parents in the town of Minchinhampton in England, Terry traveled on the Continent. He said that he turned himself over to God in the ancient Cathedral of Notre Dame in Paris. The message from the unseen Presence said: "Don't worry. I'll take care of you."

"I didn't know what that meant," Terry said, "but I knew that whatever it was, I would be all right." In calm reassurance, he returned home, and in a few months' time his and Libby's marriage was on a more solid footing than it had ever been before.

During his childhood years in Indiana, Terry had gone with his parents, Virginia Inez Collins and Gerald Layton Cosgray, and his older sister Linda Jean to the evangelical Christian Church of God in Logansport. The parents were active members, and the family attended services three or more times each week. The children received thorough grounding there in the Bible. Years later as a student in college, Terry took a tutorial course with the Jehovah's Witnesses that enabled him to build on the childhood foundation he had in knowledge of the Scriptures.

When he was eleven, the family moved to the San Francisco Bay area of California. The strong contrast of coming from a rural Midwestern area to a densely populated city made up of ethnic groups from many parts of the world offered a cultural opportunity. There were Germans and Middle Easterners, for example; and the next-door neighbors were Japanese, from whom the Cosgrays learned about Japanese food and holiday customs. When the Cosgrays first arrived in California, they continued attending the Church of God, but later they changed to the Presbyterian church. During Terry's teen years, the family attended church only rarely, going to the Catholic church for special services such as at Easter and Christmas.

Still unchurched when he went to college, Terry felt drawn to explore works on religion while he earned money shelving books in the religion section of the library. He said he dabbled in Eastern religions and read a great deal on the subject of Zen Buddhism. He became interested in the Buddhist approach to religion but felt that a genuine understanding would require years of preparation. During his exploration of Christian sects, he found what he considered a bold new religious approach to a sensitive subject in a pamphlet published by a group of English Friends, *Towards a Quaker View of Sex.* He was impressed that a church would talk frankly about this as early as the 1950s, and that their pamphlet could still be so relevant two decades later. Early in 1974, shortly after he and Libby met, they visited a midweek Friends worship group in Isla Vista to find out more about Quakerism. The Isla Vista group had been organized by Santa Barbara Monthly Meeting, and Libby and Terry were married under the care of that meeting in September 1974. Terry joined the Meeting in July 1975.

Two of Terry's acquaintances at Santa Barbara Monthly Meeting stood out in his mind as examples of persons who lived up to the Quaker ideal. One was a professor of art history, Prue Meyer. She had been disabled from childhood and walked with two canes. During a research trip to Italy she had a stroke that left her unable to speak. Undaunted, she returned home and taught the following semester by writing out her lectures and her answers to the students' questions, which were then read by a graduate student. Through sheer determination she succeeded in teaching herself to speak again and to drive a car. Her phenomenal determination to overcome handicaps and still maintain a generous spirit has been a lasting inspiration for Terry.

When their first child, Nathan, was born in Isla Vista, Libby and Terry were grateful to another good Quaker for her reassuring answer to them on how to be good parents. "Of course you will be good parents for your children," she said, "because they will be like you. They will be little Libbys and Terrys. They will be quiet, introspective types, who like to read." Terry said that has all been true!

Today they have close ties with their teenage son and daughter, who like to spend time with their parents. From the very first, when Nathan was born, Libby and Terry made the decision to take parenthood seriously and to make the welfare of their children their top priority. A lot of things have seemed important, including Terry's early ambition to have a career in creative writing, but he has put that on hold and will pursue it only when child rearing no longer requires their major attention.

Both Terry and Libby had played active roles in the Santa Barbara meeting, and both began taking on responsibilities in the Bloomington meeting soon after they started attending in early 1977. Libby has served as treasurer of the Meeting, and

Terry has been presiding clerk and has been appointed to serve on several committees. He has accepted a place on the newly appointed Fellowship committee for 1993–94.

Terry is now associate director for client services in the Office of Student Financial Assistance at Indiana University. He started working in that office while studying for a master's degree in counseling. At present he manages thirty-seven employees, some of them students, with three middle managers to assist him in dealing directly with students who need help. He says his management style is affected by his Quaker outlook.

He uses his extraordinary skills in working with people not only in his profession but also in a variety of social services. He started a mediation center in Bloomington, with the goal of helping people to settle disputes by means other than the courts — getting the parties to sit down and communicate with each other. Examples of cases he has dealt with are property division and child custody after divorces, property disputes, disputes between employers and employees, businesses in the process of dissolution, and verbal conflicts that escalate into fights.

Terry was active in the Victim-Offender Reconciliation Program, which was organized to bring perpetrators of crime together in confrontation with their victims. He says that such confrontations help the victims of crimes to deal with their pent-up emotions and their feelings of helplessness, and they bring offenders face to face with the harm they have done. Unfortunately, funding for this program has been terminated by the state of Indiana. Terry is now working with the local Citizens for Jail Improvement to find ways to restart a victim-offender reconciliation program in Bloomington.

For the past two years, Terry has enjoyed working to promote decent living conditions for mentally or physically handicapped persons through a Federal and State-funded organization, Options for Better Living. He has also been working with a group of local parents, teachers, and administrators to bring about fundamental changes in the educational program at Bloomington North High School, where Nathan and Camellia are students.

With so much of his energy spent on his multifaceted day-to-day activity, time left over for the family is precious. Their home on several wooded acres outside of Bloomington has a half-acre space for organic gardening. Tilling the soil and tending their vegetables and flowers, along with harvesting and preserving the produce, is a summer family project.

Terry experiences God everywhere. He has a daily routine that combines physical exercise, like jogging and cross-country skiing, with the spiritual exercise of meditation and directed prayer. His spiritual exercise begins with a reaffirmation of his life's priorities: personal health, marriage, family relationships, daily work, and prayers for the world. The second half of his "exercise routine" includes a less directed meditation where leadings sometimes rise out of an internal silence. Recently he has had a strong leading: "Seek first the Kingdom of God, and all these things will be added unto you." For several months he has been focusing on that verse, aware that its simplicity is deceptive, for the implications are profound.

Terry's remarkable religious journey confirms and continues the discoveries recorded over the centuries by those men and women who have lived out their lives undergirded by a profound spiritual awareness of God.

— Judy Edgerton, September 1993

QUAKER PROFILE No. 37:

Margaret Fisher Squires

We think of our interview with Peggy Squires as an outpouring of a spirit, the baring of a soul in a verbalized stream of consciousness. As she continues her spiritual journey, she finds she does not have to be in charge. Instead, she can let God take control. She says she must return to the conviction over and over again that she cannot fix all that she sees wrong every day, that she alone cannot make right all the horrors and injustices in the world.

"I couldn't do what I do if it were just me. It's God's work," she said. "If I were responsible for healing all those psychological wounds, I couldn't do it. I would cave in." She was speaking of her professional work as a psychotherapist in private practice here in Bloomington. It took years of trying too hard to do it all by herself before learning, like the Old Testament psalmist, to "cast thy burden upon the Lord, and He shall sustain thee." Her life used to be full of perfectionistic striving — what she calls "tying plastic fruit on the tree." Now, her life flows whenever she permits the help of an Indwelling Presence, which she experiences "sometimes as much as several times a month!" She says of these times, "I know God is alive, and that is what changes where the Center is, replacing my own compulsion to do things right."

She says she keeps rediscovering that God is in charge and that she doesn't have to do God's job for Him all by herself. She resists the temptation to be in complete control of her surroundings and to solve, through her own reasoning and determination, the puzzle of the suffering and evil she sees in the world.

The release from a driven life came to her as a mature person after she had been granted the Ph.D. degree in psychology from Indiana University in 1979. While performing supervised clinical work in an internship at St. Elizabeth's Hospital in Washington, D.C., she was brought face to face with the difficult problem of helping to heal wounded personalities. She was tested to the limit by those in charge at St. Elizabeth's to make sure she could stand the stress. She became unhappy and angry, and as a result decided to become a client in psychotherapy herself. Through this experience, she learned for the first time how hard she was on herself "in many subtle ways." She said she suddenly realized that the admonition to "love thy neighbor as thyself" would surely be disastrous for her, because if she was as hard on a neighbor as she was on herself, she wouldn't have a friend in the world! This was a first turn of the key to unlock the door and see inside herself that she was not expected to be perfect. She had always given lip service to a loving God, but acted as though He were demanding and critical of her.

One day, in Friends meeting in Crownsville, Maryland, during her internship at St. Elizabeth's, Peggy had an image of herself as a rigid figure standing on top of a stone base, trying hard to be good. From somewhere she suddenly became aware that she must let go, become flexible, give herself permission to make mistakes; and that this would lead her down to the ground with the less than perfect "dusty, sweaty, moving human beings." On two more occasions later, Peggy underwent counseling, each time coming to see essentially the same basic need to release the pressures on herself to be perfectly good and personally responsible for making right all the wrongs in the world.

She had a chance to begin her profession during the five years back in Bloomington from 1978 to 1983, when she was part of an addiction-treatment team at South Central Community Mental Health Center. In 1984 she was briefly on the professional staff of a mental health center in Ohio, before joining a private practice in Meadville, Pennsylvania. In that practice she found her notion of a benign God challenged by seeing the many hurting people in her practice who had been severely abused as children. "I had to make room for recognizing the amount of suffering in the world and still maintain a sense that God was good. Wrestling with that, I went to a Catholic lay leader — a spiritual person — for spiritual direction. I went through the intellectual process of trying to work out how there could be a loving God along with the evil in the world." At that time, she said, the Mary and Martha story in the New Testament came to her over and over, about how Jesus visited the home of the two sisters. She identified with Martha, the burdened one. "Always before, I had thought Jesus was saying, 'You should be more spiritual.' But I began to hear Jesus saying, 'Relax! You don't have to worry about all those things!' That was a new, liberating revelation, something in keeping with the compassionate nature of Christ — not to say, 'Mary is more spiritual, so be like her,' but instead to say, 'Don't try so hard. I am right here.'

"Then I became aware that my besetting sin was always trying to be in control, that I didn't need to intellectually understand and do all the chores just right." As she reacted to God's compassion reaching for her in this very personal way, she felt less need to intellectually reconcile the concept of a loving God with the existence of evil and suffering. She found that she could simply get on with participating in his healing work. The spiritual journeying of a Friends worship-sharing group she attends once each week has deepened this new vein of faith.

Peggy has shared her life with Michael Leslie Squires since the summer of 1970, when they were married between her junior and senior years at Earlham College in Richmond, Indiana. Another life-changing event was the birth of their daughter, Elisabeth Laura (Bethy), on May 29, 1987. At the same time Peggy was learning to care for a new little life while coping with the adult problems of clients in her practice, Mike was himself under stress in his job and was grieving for his mother, who was dying of cancer. So they both sought professional help from a therapist. Peggy says this person did a brilliant intervention for her problem of over-control. He said, "For this whole week, when you notice something you can fix or control, don't do it." She saw the usual number of things that needed to be done and people to advise, but she resisted the impulse to fix everything and found it to be a liberating experience, one that she constantly returns to.

In 1990 Bloomington Friends Meeting welcomed Peggy and Mike back, and were introduced to Bethy. The couple had known each other since Peggy was a schoolgirl traveling back to the United States after living in India. Peggy, her parents, Constance Elisabeth Clack and F. McCracken Fisher, her older brother Gordon, and her younger one, Larry, were in New Delhi from 1959 to 1964. Her father was on assignment by the United States Information Service (USIS) as a motion picture officer. Screening documentaries for release in India was among his duties. They knew their next assignment after leaving India was likely to be Ankara, Turkey, where Peggy's father would be on loan from the USIS to the Central Treaty Organization. Since Mike's father was the head of the USIS in Turkey, the Squireses invited the Fishers to a party as they passed through Ankara. Mike and Peggy met a second time later, when she was a junior in high school in Ankara. The two sets of parents knew each other well, and soon Mike's mother began addressing Peggy's mother as "mother-in-law." So the young couple declared that they had an arranged marriage!

Peggy graduated from the Air Force high school in Ankara. Her brother Gordon was already a student at Earlham College when the two of them, together with Mike, rode across Europe on the storied Orient Express on the way to Peggy's becoming an Earlham first-year student in the fall of 1966. She spent the following year, 1967–68, back in Turkey with her parents, teaching English as a foreign language at the Turkish-American Association to engineers who were preparing to go to the United States. She liked teaching, and this first job on an adult level gave her confidence as she returned to the United States for her second year at Earlham. By that time, Mike had been assigned to alternative service as a conscientious objector to war and was working in the pharmacy department at the Indiana University Medical Center in Indianapolis, so it was easy for him to visit her on weekends. They were married just before her senior year and came to Bloomington together as graduate students after her graduation from Earlham in 1971.

Peggy's childhood up to age six was spent in Arlington, Virginia, and then up to age eleven the family lived in a small suburban community near Annapolis. She describes herself as a shy child who clung to her mother in church, rather than going with other children to Sunday school at their Methodist Church. She recalls being afraid of the dark and feeling braver when her father read Bible stories to her at bedtime. So as a very young child she heard parts of the Bible read aloud, and got the message that she must "try to be good." She remembers bursting into tears, feeling that she could never be good enough, because Christ had been crucified for her.

Peggy placed the writings of C. S. Lewis, Catherine Marshall, Hannah Whitehall Smith, and Paul Tillich at the top of her list of early influences in spiritual grounding. In New Delhi, the family attended an interdenominational chapel, and her mother attended a prayer group, including Peggy in several of its meetings. Peggy recalls an elderly woman whose repeated theme was "facing God up to His promises," something that Peggy was trying to do while at the same time believing that "God is love." Peggy's mother underwent a perceptible change while attending another prayer group after returning from Turkey, becoming more relaxed and happy than she had been before. After more than two years, she told her family that she had "received the Holy Spirit" in that prayer group.

On a visit back to Turkey seventeen years ago, Peggy's parents were in a car accident and her mother was killed. Peggy feels close to her uncle Wynne Clack, who had been strongly influenced in his religious life by her mother. She has telephoned him when there have been roadblocks along the way, and says, "If you ask Uncle Wynne to pray for something, you had better be sure you want it, because you will probably get it!"

Peggy is a recognized resource person for group discussions in our Friends meeting. She is one of four leaders who helped to guide the discussion and meditation on the theme "Finding Peace, Sharing Peace" by those attending the meeting's fall retreat at Columbus Youth Camp on the eighteenth and nineteenth of last month.

Peggy finds joy in the blossoming of six-year-old Bethy, who puts her in touch day by day with the really important things in life. To know Peggy is to understand that she is indeed acquainted with the Divine Presence.

— Judy Edgerton, October 1993

QUAKER PROFILE No. 38:

Jewell Conrad Edgerton

(1909-1993...)

Readers of the first thirty-seven of these profiles are bound to be disappointed by the abrupt change of authors at this point. They may also be impatient with the substitute author's inability to keep himself out of Judy's story. He did try, but Judy's life and his were so intertwined for more than sixty-one years that the effort was bound to fail. He asks readers to be patient. As for the fact that Judy's profile is twice as long as any of the others, this needs no defense. Judy is the only person profiled in this book who no longer has any opportunity to add new pages to her profile.

* * *

Jewell Conrad (Judy) Edgerton was endowed with two great talents. She had a glorious coloratura voice, and she had a remarkable gift as a writer. She lacked just one thing that appears to be indispensable for a successful career in any of the arts: an irrepressible ego. Judy often said, "We have to make choices." Throughout her life, Judy made choices that placed other people's interests and welfare ahead of her own.

Jewell Mock Conrad was born and grew up in a country setting just west of Winston-Salem, in the North Carolina Piedmont. The hardships and destruction of the Civil War were still fresh in the memories of her grandparents. Some relatives on both sides of her family had left North Carolina after the Civil War and settled in Indiana. During Judy's childhood her North Carolina relatives looked on Indiana as a kind of Promised Land.

The strait-laced Mocks, the family of Judy's mother, Pearl, were substantial and respected members of their farming community, but Judy always thought the less well-off Conrads got more enjoyment out of life. Pearl graduated from high school, finished her education at Salem Teachers' Institute, and taught school for several years before she met handsome Virgil W. Conrad, a man ten years her senior who was known to his friends as Bob. He had spent some years working in Texas and Indiana before returning to the community where he had grown up. In an autobiography written late in life for her children, Judy's mother said: "Bob and I were married in 1908 against my parents' consent." They settled down on the farm that Bob Conrad had bought two years earlier, "which he told me he bought because he knew I would never be satisfied any place but a farm," Judy's mother added, "but I could have been satisfied in any place with that little man." For some time after their daughter's marriage, the Mock parents refused to visit the young couple. The family says that Philip Mock's opposition melted away when he became seriously ill and his son-in-law Bob Conrad looked after him all through his illness.

Life was very hard for Bob and Pearl during the first years on their farm. Both of them worked together in the fields, and after Judy was born they would take her with them before she was six years old to look after first one and then a second baby brother. In later life Judy said she had never known what it was to have a carefree childhood. By the time her two sisters, Virgie and Madge, came along, their father's industry and good business sense had made the farm so productive and their home so comfortable that the younger girls had no idea how hard life had been for their parents during those early years.

Judy inherited her father's keen, independent mind and his organizing ability, along with her mother's serious temperament and capacity for hard work. Unfortunately, she also inherited her father's weak heart. During the latter years of her life she often remarked that she knew her heart would eventually be the cause of her death.

She was an excellent student in high school, and her teachers encouraged her to go on to college. After graduation she took a short business course and spent the next two years working in an office in nearby Winston-Salem, but she still wanted a college education. Somebody suggested that she get in touch with Guilford College, a Quaker institution only thirty miles from her home, and so she did. To the very end of her life she remained grateful that President Raymond Binford gave her the opportunity to earn her way through Guilford by working as a secretary in the college offices. She once said that holding a practically full-time office job had given her little opportunity to get more than a superficial education. Her record shows otherwise, however. She was on the honor roll in her freshman and senior years, vice-president of the class in her freshman year, and president of Women's Student Government in her senior year. In her junior year she won the William F. Overman Scholarship, awarded annually to the junior who had contributed the most to college life while excelling academically.

Judy had grown up in the Olivet Moravian Church, which stood within scarcely more than a mile of the Conrad family farm, and she loved the musical heritage of the Moravians. At Guilford the director of the college choir was quick to discover her remarkable voice, and he began giving her vocal lessons. She was the choir soloist during her last three years in college. She attracted a good deal of favorable attention on the choir's annual spring concert tours through the northeastern states, which in 1931 included a performance for President Hoover on the White House lawn. In the 1932 spring concert tour, now a junior, she also attracted a good deal of favorable attention from a freshman tenor in the choir whose name was Bill Edgerton. On that tour they fell deeply in love with each other.

During her college years Judy had neither the time nor the inclination to seek an active social life. But soon after they returned from the choir tour, Bill discovered that he had a rival — an older distant cousin of his. Joe (not his real name) had been teaching and coaching at a nearby high school since his graduation from Guilford the year before Judy entered. He and Judy appeared to have little in common. Joe had been an outstanding athlete in college, and she cared nothing for sports. Judy loved music, and he had no interest in music. But after two years of casual dating in the midst of her heavy schedule of classes and office work, Judy had begun to go along with Joe's assumption that they would eventually be married.

In the spring of Bill's freshman year, Joe was awarded a full scholarship at Haverford College in Pennsylvania to work for a master's degree in the following year. With Bill now on the scene, Joe became nervous about what might happen in his absence. During his first semester at Haverford, he came home twice and tried to persuade Judy to marry him immediately. During the spring tour of the Guilford Choir he followed her from concert to concert in the Philadelphia area with a marriage license and wedding ring in hand. Once he took Judy and her roommate for an automobile ride along with a friend of his own and suddenly stopped the car before the door of a justice of the peace. Judy refused to get out of the car.

That was a year of anguish for Judy. She saw that the three of them were caught in a triangle where there was no satisfactory solution for all three. After she and Bill discovered each other, she could not continue to think of marrying Joe, and yet all winter she had been unable to give him an outright rejection for fear of its possible effect on his strenuous graduate program at Haverford. She also feared that rejecting Joe might make Bill feel a moral obligation to marry her when he had completed his education, regardless of how he might be inclined by that time.

What especially worried Judy was the calendar difference in their ages. When Bill first met her, he had no idea she was nearly five years older than he. When she told him, he said that since he hadn't noticed the difference, that proved it didn't matter. Then he started a list of happily married couples with at least as great a difference in their ages, beginning with the poets Robert and Elizabeth Barrett Browning (six years); George Fox, the founder of Quakerism, and his wife Margaret Fell (ten years); and a number of less famous people among Bill's and Judy's personal acquaintances. Bill finally convinced her that he was serious about wanting to spend the rest of his life with her, regardless of what the calendar said. He argued that counting the years was an inexact way of calculating a person's real age. (The photo of her published in this book bears him out. No one has ever come close to guessing that Judy was fifty-eight years old when that photograph was made.)

Toward the end of the choir tour Joe's desperate effort to avoid losing Judy finally led to the very thing he was struggling to prevent. Judy rejected him completely. Before the year was out, he married a fellow teacher in his high school, a fine young woman who had much more in common with him than Judy did. But years later, tender-hearted Judy still acknowledged a feeling of guilt for whatever role her rejection might have played in his failure to get his master's degree.

During Bill's senior year at Guilford he won the same full scholarship for Haverford College that his cousin had won two years earlier. An important subject of his and Judy's daily exchange of letters during his year at Haverford was how they could arrange to get married as soon as he received his M.A. Suddenly, in April 1935, the new headmaster of Perkiomen School in Pennsylvania, who had known both of them at Guilford, offered Judy a job as his secretary and offered Bill a job teaching French and German. They were married in June and started work at Perkiomen four days later.

After spending two years at Perkiomen School, Judy and Bill were desperate to get out of jobs that appeared to hold little promise for the future. In their naïveté they thought wondrous opportunities would open up for them if Bill accepted an appointment to spend a year in a French lycée as an assistant in English and Judy spent that year continuing her study with a superb voice teacher she had recently discovered in Philadelphia. She got a good secretarial position with the Girard Life Insurance Company, across the street from historic Independence Hall; and under the guidance of Berta Levina, who had sung leading roles with the old Philadelphia Opera Company, she learned how to use her voice so well that it retained its beauty and power to the very end of her life. Bill came home from France with fluent French, but the only job opportunity it led to was a very modest position in a private school for girls near Philadelphia. The following year when Guilford invited him to come back and teach

French, he and Judy reluctantly accepted even though it cost Judy the opportunity to continue her voice study with Berta Levina.

The birth of their daughter Susan four months after their return to Guilford left Judy with almost no time for music during their first year there. By early 1941, however, Greensboro musical circles were taking notice of her. From March 1941 till April 1942 she was the soloist in a weekly program of classical music on the principal radio station in Greensboro. Encouraged by her reception on that program, she took two months off during the summer and returned to Philadelphia for further study with Berta Levina. Invitations to sing continued to come in after she got back home. During Bill's eight years on the Guilford College faculty, from 1939 till 1947, she was the soprano soloist in a number of performances of Handel's *Messiah* and was in demand with other choral groups as well as in various churches.

Along with their excitement over Judy's musical successes and over the development of little Susan, Judy and Bill were also troubled by the steadily expanding Second World War. In the midst of Nazi aggression their wavering faith in Christian and Quaker peace principles was bolstered in 1941 by their reading of *The Power of Nonviolence*, by Richard Gregg, and *War Without Violence*, by Krishnalal Shridharani, both of them personal acquaintances and followers of Gandhi. Unfortunately, the stand Bill and Judy took together on the peace testimony turned out in the end to be much more costly for Judy than for Bill. In the spring of 1944, the local draft board sent Bill a first notification of a possible call-up, which in his case would have led to assignment to a Civilian Public Service camp for conscientious objectors to war. Almost simultaneously, the way opened for him to go overseas for two years of war-relief work with the American Friends Service Committee. Assignment to a CPS camp would probably have meant forest service in some camp close enough for occasional short visits to Judy and their two small children, but overseas war-relief work offered the prospect of doing something that promised to be more useful. Not once did Judy question the second choice. For two long, lonely years she shouldered the full burden of care for their two children in the little house they occupied on the Guilford College campus. Bill's war relief work kept him busy in Egypt for a year of work among 25,000 Yugoslavs — refugees from the German invaders of their country. He then spent six months in postwar Germany helping children who had been taken out of their native countries by the Nazi occupants. Finally, in his last five months, he co-organized the Anglo-American Quaker relief program in Poland. All through those two years, Judy allowed no hint of the strain she was under to creep into her invariably cheerful letters. Not till long after Bill returned home in 1946 did he begin to comprehend how lonely and difficult those years had been for his wife.

Bill came home so concerned about the problem of an expansionist Soviet Russia that he wanted to make a major career change. Judy readily agreed. In 1947 he resigned his position at Guilford College, and they set out with eight-year-old Susan and four-year-old David for Shanks Village, the Federal housing project on the other side of the Hudson River from Columbia University. They lived there for the next two and a half years while Bill completed his Ph.D. residence requirement in Russian studies.

As a Federal housing project, Shanks Village was open to qualified families without regard to race. In 1948, their neighbors in Shanks Village got up in arms upon learning that a poor black family whose house had burned down was going to be moved into the apartment next door. In racial matters, Judy was endowed with Christian color blindness. She calmly told all their neighbors, "Now, look here, we're a Southern family, and we expect you Northerners to set us a good example!"

Bill's fifteen hundred dollar fellowship, the best Columbia had to offer, proved to be not nearly enough to meet their expenses, and during the first semester Judy added to the family income by typing graduate students' term papers and theses — often working all night long. They were saved just in time when the American Council of Learned Societies offered a fabulous new fellowship to encourage graduate work in Russian studies. When Bill went for an interview with the family budget in hand, the interviewer said: "I don't see how you are living." Bill replied, "I don't either." They got the fellowship.

Upon Bill's completion of his course work for the Ph.D. at the beginning of 1950, they spent the next nine years as a typical migrating faculty family, five of them in the heart of Pennsylvania at the Pennsylvania State University. There they were active in State College Friends Meeting. Son David still has glowing memories of his mother as "the best First-day school teacher I ever had — friendly, charming, funny, with a carefully-planned lesson that always caught and kept kids' attention." She was constantly in demand as a soloist in the Presbyterian and Baptist churches, and she would often perform double duty on Sundays, hurrying away after teaching First-day school to sing for the Presbyterians or the Baptists. She also contributed to the family income at Penn State by serving on call as an emergency office worker whenever and wherever needed — a job that gave her an interesting insight into the workings of the whole university.

Judy and Bill never lived in North Carolina after 1947, and their children spent practically all their school years in New York, Pennsylvania, and the Midwest; but all of them were conscious of their roots in the red clay soil of piedmont North Carolina. Almost every summer and many Christmases, all four of them would go "back home" to the Conrad family farm. One of David's most memorable visits was the summer he spent at the age of fourteen working on the farm with his Uncle Philip, who taught him how to cultivate a field with the family's full-size John Deere tractor. David grows downright lyrical as he recalls the effect of those visits on Judy: "Mother's speech would actually change as the redness of the clay deepened on those trips south. She was a natural at 'code-switching' between her role as a Northern faculty wife and her origins as a profoundly Southern woman with rich rural roots. Those long visits south — 'back home' to Mother — enlivened and strengthened her. She seemed almost to draw spiritual nourishment from them. I remember she could do more than just sing Mozart and Handel with that wonderful voice: she could let out a thunderous Tarheel hog-call — 'Sooo-EEEEEEEEE!' Sometimes her brother Gordon would say: 'Come on, Judy, let's call the hogs,' just to hear her do it."

David also recalls the summer when they combined their annual trip to North Carolina with attending the annual Friends General Conference at Cape May, New Jersey, where Judy and another mother "team-taught us kids First-day school, or keep-the-kids-busy school, or whatever it was. One day a couple of boys at the back of the room took it into their heads to see if they could disconcert the teachers by making un-Quakerly boys' gun and hand-grenade noises — you know, *kksssh, kksssh, puh-khhh.* The other mother got satisfyingly disconcerted for them; but Mom just grinned, pointed an imaginary finger pistol, and shot back at them — it shut 'em right up."

Bill's two years of Quaker-sponsored relief work led to so many proposals for further Quaker work after the war that Judy used to joke about never being jealous of other women: she was jealous only of the American Friends Service Committee! And with good reason — Bill was constantly asked to speak and write on AFSC work abroad and to participate in AFSC institutes, international seminars, publications, and overseas missions. On rare occasions the whole family was able to share the trips within the United States. One summer when Bill served as a visiting discussion leader at several AFSC international seminars, the whole family had an exciting adventure traveling in their little Austin from Woodstock, Vermont, to Milton, Massachusetts, to Guilford College in North Carolina, and as far west as Beloit College in Wisconsin.

But out of Bill's forty-one visits to Europe on either Quaker work or professional work, Judy was able to share only three: a dreary semester in Russia in 1963, relieved before and after by a ride on the Orient Express from Germany to Bulgaria and by brief visits in western Europe; a wonderful trip to Italy, Germany, and England in 1972; and a memorable visit in 1983 to their son David and his family when they were living in Kenya, with a pleasant stop in England on their way home. Most of Bill's trips alone were short, but they added up to a loss of more than four of their fifty-eight years of married life on this earth.

Judy and Bill did have one exciting joint adventure in Quaker work. In the spring of 1968 they spent four months working with the Friends Committee on National Legislation as "Friends in Washington." Bill's task was to try to interpret the complexities of Soviet Russia and Communist-dominated Eastern Europe to Congress, and Judy served as his appointments secretary. It was agreed that they should concentrate on the newer members of the House of Representatives from the Southern states, where their Southern background and accent might help them to open doors and minds. In the 86 Congressional working days of their four-month stay, Bill had at least one interview with 79 members of Congress and their staffs, who represented 31 of the 50 states in the Union. Judy's effectiveness can be judged from the comment of a Representative from the deep South after an excellent interview lasting an hour and a quarter: "You may be interested to know how you got this appointment. It was just that your wife had such a ni-i-ice vo-i-ce. You'd better make good use of her while you're here. Tell her I said so." This was the only time in their lives that Judy and Bill had an opportunity to work together in a Quaker project of national importance. She often said she wished Bill's work could have kept him close enough to Washington for her to volunteer her time regularly at FCNL.

In 1958, Bill was invited to join the Indiana University faculty as chairman of the rapidly expanding Slavic department, and the family settled permanently in Bloomington. Judy cheerfully took on the responsibility for departmental entertaining, along with her social concerns in the town and her religious concerns in Bloomington Friends Meeting. She was always a strong supporter of Monroe County United Ministries and its wide-ranging program of social services to low-income families. Beginning soon after the Edgertons' arrival in Bloomington, she worked for several years as a volunteer driver for the Head Start program for preschool children.

Judy was a feminist long before feminism became fashionable. She often recalled with quiet indignation the disadvantages and discrimination that little girls were subjected to in her childhood. She had no patience with men who exploited women or denied them equal rights, and her impatience extended all the way from Lot's attitude toward his own daughters in the Old Testament and Paul's attitude toward women in the New, to the wife-beating and child-abusing men of our own day. When she became eligible for Social Security, she opened a separate checking account to receive her benefits. Her check stubs for that account are a history of Judy's social concerns and quiet generosity. Along with helping children and grandchildren get through occasional financial difficulties, she contributed regularly and generously to the protection of women's rights and to the support of promising women candidates for political office.

In Bloomington Judy again placed the opportunities for her family ahead of her own advancement in singing. Occasionally she would desert her nonmusical Quaker meeting for worship on Sunday mornings to serve as a guest soloist in some mainline Protestant church, but for the most part her growing contribution to our Friends meeting came at the cost of her almost complete sacrifice of her God-given talent in music.

At the beginning of 1991, she found an inspiring voice teacher in Bloomington, Ethel Closson Smith, and she continued taking lessons with her up to the time of her death. Dr. Smith used Judy as a model to demonstrate to her other pupils that the person who has learned to use her voice properly can preserve its power and beauty well into her eighties. At the time of her death, Judy was looking forward to spending the first months of 1994 preparing the beautiful motet "Exsultate, jubilate . . .," which Mozart, her favorite composer, had written at the age of seventeen.

This narrative would be seriously incomplete if it took no account of the long interval during which Judy and Bill were able to play almost no part in Bloomington Meeting. For some ten years between the early 1970s and Judy's resumption of editing the newsletter in April 1990, she and Bill went through the kind of family tragedy that has only very recently come to be discussed in public. It involved abuse of two generations by a husband and father. Judy and Bill's two children had grown up in an environment in which family violence, child abuse, and broken marriages were unknown. Paradoxically, such a tranquil environment can sometimes make it difficult for a sensitive child to cope with previously unknown dangers. Judy and Bill finally succeeded in helping their daughter escape from her marriage, but they ultimately failed to rescue her three children permanently even after three court trials.

One of Judy's strong concerns was for the care and spiritual growth of the children in Bloomington Meeting. Soon after her arrival she played an active role in First-day school. Following Judy's death, one young mother commented: "I am grateful for many things, but especially the concern and love Judy showed to the children of our Meeting, frequently offering wonderful spoken messages which have made the young ones feel included in a way not easily achievable in that first fifteen minutes of worship before the children withdraw for their own session." Two mothers of small children expressed gratitude for Judy's way of drawing even the youngest into the life of the Meeting by giving them some little responsibility in connection with refreshments.

Judy was impatient with slipshod work. When she served for a year as clerk of Bloomington Meeting's social committee, she set as her first goal the establishment of an orderly procedure for handling meals and refreshments for special Meeting occasions, posting brief notes in strategic places in the meeting's inconveniently small kitchen to guide those who would take over after her term of service. She also finally persuaded the Meeting to abandon its vestige of pagan liberty and start every meal at the meetinghouse by standing in a circle and holding hands, grownups and children together, for a few moments of silent thanks before going through the meal line.

When several members lost close relatives a few years before her own death, Judy invited them to gather at the Edgerton home for an evening of sharing and coping together with their bereavement. "I was so impressed," one of them said, "by her loving and spiritual approach to this difficult and powerful experience." She recalled Judy's consoling comment that those of us who were fortunate enough to have close and loving ties are naturally the ones who experience the loss most keenly.

Perhaps the most lasting monument to Judy's memory in Bloomington Friends Meeting will be the thirty-seven Quaker profiles in this volume which she published as editor of the

Meeting's newsletter from 1990 until her death in December 1993. It should not be overlooked, however, that she had also won appreciation many years earlier for her first stint as editor of the newsletter. A typical response came in November 1974 from the late Bill Dietz, who with his wife Mig played a leading role in the Meeting for years, even though they lived thirty-five miles away: "You will recall it was Judy's fine authorship of the newsletter that really attracted us to Bloomington."

Readers of the first thirty-seven profiles in this book will no doubt be surprised at the following words found after Judy's death in notes for her own profile: "I've never considered myself to be much of a Quaker. I wasn't born into it, nor 'convinced,' really; I just wandered into it by marrying one of those bona fide genuine English-ancestry types." Judy came into the Society of Friends from the outside, but without the disillusionment and rebellion against a previous religious affiliation that is often found among newcomers to Quakerism. By the time she became a Friend at Guilford in the early 1940s, her life had already been enriched by contacts with enough other religious denominations to make her aware that none of them has a monopoly on truth — not even any of the splintered groups that share the Quaker label. Her religious faith was strong, independent, and ecumenical. Her inner life was a continuous journey of spiritual exploration. The Quaker emphasis on direct and continuing revelation was a source of great strength and freedom for her. It enabled her to approach the Bible reverently without subjecting it to idolatry. She was solidly grounded in our Christian heritage, but she was open to new light from any direction. She could have called herself a Christ-centered universalist. Along with valuing the strengths of the Society of Friends, she also recognized one great weakness: its failure to appreciate the spiritual value of music. In unprogrammed Quaker meetings she missed the rich musical tradition of the German Moravians.

Death crept up on Judy when she was at the height of her creative powers. The last five years of her life were a strange period of struggle between forces that seemed bent on taking her away from us and forces that offered the promise of greater physical health than she had known for years. This was also a period when she and Bill were glimpsing new vistas in their exploration of spiritual reality. In the final years of their life together, devotional reading every morning became a joyous part of their daily routine. They reread Thomas Kelly's *Testament of Devotion* and discovered his later collection of writings edited by his son, *The Eternal Promise*. They found a treasure in the well-known anthology published by London Yearly Meeting, *Christian Faith and Practice in the Experience of the Society of Friends*. With the help of the *Abingdon Bible Commentary*, and the lively little book *Rescuing the Bible from Fundamentalism* by the Episcopal bishop John Shelby Spong, they started systematically rediscovering and rereading the Bible, book by book. And along with all those volumes they kept coming back to a religious work that they had reread more often during the previous thirty years than any other book except the Bible itself. It is *The Christian Agnostic* by the prominent English Methodist Leslie D. Weatherhead. Once again they marveled that so few Quakers appear to be familiar with a book that, with a few minor exceptions, is so Quakerly in its ideas and spirit.

The expressions of grief and gratitude and love since her death show that Judy's most important contribution to Bloomington Meeting came in numerous quiet acts of personal encouragement and support. "Hers was a special warm presence in our Meeting and in our lives," said one member, "welcoming and encouraging us all." Another said: "I remember her generous spirit — her willingness to hug, to put her arm around someone, to take another's hand in welcome or consolation." And still another said, "Judy was a wonderful example of pure Christianity in thought and action. It was a joy to be in the same room with her."

Judy and Bill had long been interested in serious studies of psychic phenomena. Several years before her death, they agreed that when the first of them died they would both make every possible effort to communicate with each other. Five days after Judy's death, a member of Bloomington Meeting, Barbara Bolz, called Bill up and told him about Judy's appearance to her in a remarkable lucid dream. She said the sharp, clear pictures in that dream contrasted strongly with the fuzzy pictures of her ordinary dreams. At Bill's urgent request she wrote the dream down immediately, while it was fresh in her memory. The scene of the dream was what is called in Bloomington Meeting the piano room, a small room between the entrance hall and the kitchen where Meeting members who especially like religious music gather every Sunday and sing informally for half an hour just before the regular meeting for worship. Judy felt a special responsibility for preparing refreshments to be served after meeting, and she would sometimes sing along from the kitchen before coming in and joining the rest of the singers. Here is Barbara Bolz's letter:

> Last night I had the most beautiful dream about Judy. I was singing in the piano room with Marci Ankrom when I heard Judy's unmistakable voice coming from the kitchen. I said to Marci, "That sounds like Judy in there," and she responded, "It *is* Judy." I looked at Marci and said, a bit perplexed, "But Judy died." Marci replied, "I know." I stood up and walked into the kitchen where Judy was standing, a bit stooped over, drying a plate. She looked exactly like I last saw her, except she had a very slight glow about her (nothing too overstated, just a warmth and a glow). She looked up at me and her eyes sparkled with love. I asked, "Judy, how is it?" (meaning death), and she answered, "It's wonderful, dear, just wonderful." I said, "Judy, please, please visit Bill in a dream like this one." She looked far off and said, "I love him." I said, "I know you do, but please visit him." She then looked right into my eyes and spoke to me as if she were answering my request. She spoke directly to me and said slowly, with a great deal of meaning in her voice: *"I love him."*

— William Edgerton

BOOKS AND PAMPHLETS MENTIONED IN THESE PROFILES

Abingdon Bible Commentary, ed. Frederick Carl Eiselen, Edwin Lewis, and David G. Downey. Nashville, Tenn.: Abingdon Press, 1929.

Barclay's Apology in Modern English, ed. Dean Freiday, 3rd ptg., 1980. Obtainable from Friends Book Store, Philadelphia; Quaker Hill Book Store, Richmond, Ind.; and other bookstores.

Bhagavad-Gita, trans. Franklin Edgerton. Cambridge, Mass.: Harvard University Press, 1944.

Boulding, Elise. *Born Remembering*. Pendle Hill Pamphlet No. 200. Wallingford, Penna., 1975.

Brinton, Howard. *Friends for 300 Years: The History and Beliefs of the Society of Friends since George Fox Started the Movement*. New York: Harper & Brothers, 1952.

Brommell, Anna Pettit. *A Quaker Story Caravan*. Wallingford, Penna.: Pendle Hill Publications, 1935; paperback: 1962.

Brother Lawrence. *The Practice of the Presence of God*. Editions still in print from: White Plains, N.Y.: Peter Pauper Press, 1967; Grand Rapids, Mich.: Revell, 1980; Uhrichsville, Ohio: Barbour & Co., 1993.

Chrétien de Troyes. *Perceval, or the Story of the Holy Grail*. New York: Elsevier Science, Inc. (Pergamon Press), 1981.

Christian Faith and Practice in the Experience of the Society of Friends. London: London Yearly Meeting, 1960, 1988.

Cooper, Wilmer A. *A Living Faith: An Historical Study of Quaker Beliefs*. Richmond, Ind.: Friends United Press, 1990.

Course in Miracles, A. Various editions still in print from: Glen Ellen, Calif.: Foundation for Inner Peace, 1975–1992.

Dante Alighieri. *The Divine Comedy*. Numerous editions in English translation.

Dostoyevsky, Fyodor. "The Grand Inquisitor," a long chapter in *The Brothers Karamazov*. (Recommended: the Garnett-Matlaw English translation, New York: W. W. Norton, 1976.)

Elliott, Errol. *Quakers on the American Frontier*. Richmond, Ind.: Friends United Press, 1969.

Ellwood, Thomas. *The History of the Life of Thomas Ellwood*, ed. C. S. Crump. London, 1900.

Fox, George. *The Journal*, ed. John L. Nickalls (a rev. ed.). London: Religious Society of Friends, 1975. Available from the Quaker Hill Book Store, Richmond, Ind.

Fox, Matthew. *Original Blessing*. Santa Fe, N.M.: Bear and Co., 1983.

Gregg, Richard. *The Power of Nonviolence*, 3rd ed. Canton, Maine: Greenleaf Books, 1984.

Hammarskjöld, Dag. *Markings*. New York: Knopf, 1964; paperback: Ballantine (Epiphany Books), 1985.

Hartog, Jan de. *The Peaceable Kingdom: An American Saga*. New York: Atheneum, 1972.

Holmes, Ernest. *How to Use the Science of Mind*. New York: Putnam Publishing Group, 1989.

Holmes, Ernest. *Living the Science of Mind*. New York: Putnam Publishing Group, 1991.

Jones, Rufus. *The Double Search: Studies in Atonement and Prayer*. Philadelphia: John C. Winston Co., 1906.

Kelly, Thomas. *Testament of Devotion*. Harper-San Francisco, 1992 (reprint of 1941 edition).

Kelly, Thomas. *The Eternal Promise*, 2nd ed. Richmond, Ind.: Friends United Press, 1988.

Kenworthy, Leonard. *Quakerism: A Study Guide on the Religious Society of Friends*. Dublin, Ind.: Prinit Press, 1981.

MacLeish, Archibald. *J.B.: A Play in Verse*. New York: Houghton-Mifflin, 1958.

Merton, Thomas. *The Hidden Ground of Love: The Letters of Thomas Merton*. New York: Farrar, Straus & Giroux, 1985.

Mullen, Tom. *Where Two or Three Are Gathered Together, Someone Spills the Milk*. Richmond, Ind.: Friends United Press, 1986.

Mullen, Thomas. *Laughing Out Loud and Other Religious Experiences.* Richmond, Ind.: Friends United Press, 1989.

Shetter, Janette K. *Rhythms of the Ecosystem*. Pendle Hill Pamphlet No. 208. Wallingford, Penna., 1976.

Shridharani, Krishnalal. *War Without Violence: A Study of Gandhi's Method and Its Accomplishments.* New York: Harcourt, Brace, 1939.

Spong, Bishop John Shelby. *Rescuing the Bible from Fundamentalism: A Bishop Rethinks the Meaning of Scripture.* Harper-San Francisco, 1991; paperback: 1992.

Tolles, Frederick. *Meetinghouse and Counting House: The Quaker Merchants of Colonial Philadelphia, 1682–1763.* Chapel Hill, N.C.: University of North Carolina Press, 1948.

Towards a Quaker View of Sex: An Essay by a Group of Friends, rev. limited ed., London: Friends Home Service Committee, 1963, 1964.

Underhill, Evelyn. *Mysticism.* Paperback: New York: NAL-Dutton, 1934; New York: Doubleday, 1990.

Weatherhead, Leslie D. *The Christian Agnostic*. London: Hodder and Stoughton, 1965. Paperback: Nashville, Tenn.: Abingdon Press, 1990.

West, Jessamyn. *The Quaker Reader.* Wallingford, Penna.: Pendle Hill Publications, 1992.

Woolman, John. *The Journal and Major Essays,* ed. Phillips P. Moulton. Oxford University Press, 1971.

Youngblut, John. *On Hallowing One's Diminishments.* Pendle Hill Pamphlet No. 292. Wallingford, Penna., 1990.